THEOPHRASTUS

METAPHYSICS

THEOPHRASTUS
METAPHYSICS

ΘΕΟΦΡΑΣΤΟΥ

ΤΩΝ ΜΕΤΑ ΤΑ ΦΥΣΙΚΑ

Greek Text
with Facing English Translation,
Introduction and Commentary

by

W. D. ROSS and F. H. FOBES

CONTENTS

INTRODUCTION	ix
TEXT AND TRANSLATION	2
COMMENTARY	41
INDEXES	
Index verborum	77
Index to the Introduction and Commentary	84

PREFACE

THE present work owes its origin to the editors' belief that, in attempting to establish the text of a work so difficult as the *Metaphysica*, careful regard should be paid to the oldest known MS., the *Vindobonensis*. This MS. was for some reason neglected even in the valuable edition of the late Hermann Usener. The editors had hoped that a recollation of Usener's MSS., together with a collation of the *Vindobonensis* and of all the late MSS., might result in a clear understanding of their interrelations and might thus give a firm basis for reconstituting the text on other than eclectic principles. In this hope they have been to some extent disappointed, though it does indeed appear that Usener's MSS. are not fairly representative of the tradition.

The text as here given, the English translation, the greater part of the Introduction, and all the Commentary are the work of Mr. Ross; for that part of the Introduction which deals with the MSS., for the *apparatus criticus*, and for the Indexes Mr. Fobes is responsible.

The editors are under obligation to Professor Rostagno of the Laurentian Library, and to the other librarians mentioned in the Introduction (p. xxvii), for their courteous and painstaking assistance. They owe much to the members of the Oxford Aristotelian Society, whose study of the *Metaphysica* in 1904 furnished Mr. Ross with many valuable suggestions. They wish also to acknowledge their indebtedness to the Delegates of the Press for undertaking the publication of the book, and to the staff of the Press for their helpful advice and for their vigilant supervision of details.

W. D. R.
F. H. F.

INTRODUCTION

ALL the Greek manuscripts of this work assign it to Theophrastus. A scholion at the end adds that it was unknown to Hermippus (c. 200 B.C.) and to Andronicus (c. 85 B.C.) and does not occur in their lists of Theophrastus' writings, but that Nicolaus (i.e. Nicolaus of Damascus) ascribed it to Theophrastus. Thus the tradition that Theophrastus was its author goes back to about 25 B.C. The parallels which Usener[1] points out between 8^b 6-9 and Theophrastus' *Physicae Opiniones* fr. 8 (Diels, *Dox.* 483. 11-484. 18) and between 9^b 1-5, 21-4 and *Phys. Opin.* fr. 10 (ib. 485. 6-16) are not very striking. But the writer takes account, as Theophrastus would have done, of the history of Greek philosophy down to Aristotle, and of nothing later; the philosophical outlook agrees with what we know of Theophrastus; and there is nothing in the style or vocabulary that need make us doubt the correctness of Nicolaus' ascription.

The title τὰ μετὰ τὰ φυσικά must have been imposed on the work at some time after Andronicus' edition of Aristotle's works, from which the phrase took its origin; and may have been imposed by Nicolaus, who was the first, so far as we know, to refer to Aristotle's *Metaphysics* by that name. In a manuscript of the Antonian Library at Padua (Scaff. xvii. 370, of the thirteenth century) there is a Latin translation of the work headed ' Incipit liber Aristotelis de principiis translatus de graeco in latinum a Magistro Bartholomaeo de Messana in curia illustrissimi Manfredi Serenissimi Regis Siciliae scientiae amatoris, de mandato suo'; and V. Rose thinks[2] that the book is to be identified with the περὶ ἀρχῶν ἢ φύσεως ᾱ which occurs in Hesychius' list of Aristotle's works, and with the περὶ ἀρχῆς which occurs in Diogenes' list. If this be so, Hermippus did not mention it in his list of

[1] *Kleine Schriften*, i. 92 = *Rh. Mus.* 1861. 260.
[2] *Arist. Pseudep.* 183.

Theophrastus' works simply because he wrongly included it in his list of *Aristotle's* works, on which that of Diogenes is probably based. But it seems unlikely that Hermippus would have failed to notice the obviously unaristotelian character of the work. It is far more likely that the περὶ ἀρχῆς which he ascribed to Aristotle is the first book of our *Physics*, and that the mistake of the Padua manuscript is of much later origin.

Krische[1] identified this work with the περὶ τῶν ἁπλῶν διαπορημάτων which occurs in Diogenes' list of Theophrastus' works,[2] a list which (unlike his list of Aristotle's writings) was probably based on that of Andronicus.[3] But the identification is manifestly highly improbable, nor is there any other of Diogenes' titles with which one is tempted to connect the work. In any case, Usener is probably right in saying that the author of the scholion (or his authority) had satisfied himself not only that the title τὰ μετὰ τὰ φυσικά did not occur in the early lists of Theophrastus' writings, but that the contents of the 'Fragment' did not correspond with anything represented in these lists. On the other hand it is incorrect to say, as J. G. Schneider does, that Hermippus and Andronicus rejected the treatise as not being the genuine work of Theophrastus. They simply did not know of its existence.

The manuscripts describe the work as Θεοφράστου τῶν μετὰ τὰ φυσικά, as *part* of Theophrastus' *Metaphysics*, and it is commonly now described as the 'Metaphysical Fragment'; but this is somewhat misleading. The work is short enough, but appears to be a complete essay preliminary to a fuller metaphysical work, very much as is Book B of Aristotle's *Metaphysics*; and there is no evidence that Theophrastus ever got further.

The essay is printed in the *editio princeps* of Aristotle (Aldus, 1498); in the edition of Theophrastus published at Basel in 1541 by Hieronymus Gemusaeus or Oporinus (a

---

[1] *Die theolog. Lehren der griechischen Denker*, 343.
[2] D. L. v. 46.
[3] E. Howald, in *Hermes*, 1920. 204-21, has offered good grounds for holding that it is based on Andronicus rather than on Hermippus.

reprint of the Aldine), and in a reprint of this (bearing the same date) in which Priscian's *Metaphrasis* is added; in the Camotian Aristotle (Venice, 1552), and in the Sylburg Aristotle (Frankfurt, 1585). It is omitted in the edition of Theophrastus' shorter works by H. Stephanus (Paris, 1557), in the editions of Theophrastus by Furlanus and Turnebus (Hanover, 1605), by Daniel Heinsius (Leyden, 1613), and by J. G. Schneider (Leipzig, 1818-21), but was printed by Brandis[1] with Aristotle's *Metaphysics* (Berlin, 1823), and in Wimmer's two editions of Theophrastus (Leipzig, 1862, and Paris, 1866), and finally has been edited separately by H. Usener (Bonn, 1890). It is the subject of a Greek commentary by Camotius (Venice, 1551).

The essay begins by asking how the scope of metaphysics ('the study of first things') is to be delimited. This study is commonly distinguished from the study of nature as being something that deals with what is unchanging, and is therefore said to deal with objects of reason, not of sense (4^a 2-9). The first question to be considered is whether the two classes of objects are related to one another or are quite separate elements in reality. It is to be presumed that they are in relation and that the objects of reason are principles prior to and presupposed by the objects of sense (4^a 9-17). Where then are they to be found? If (1) they are to be identified with the objects of mathematics, the objection arises that the connexion of these with objects of sense is not very clear, and that they are hardly worthy of the position assigned to them, being creations of the human mind; or if not this, at all events not well qualified to impart life and motion to the things of sense (4^a 17-^{b} 5). If (2) they are identified with something prior in nature to the objects of mathematics, we must try to specify whether this is one in number, species, or genus. It will probably be found only in a few things, and perhaps only in the first or highest reality. It is presumably to be described as differing from all other things by superiority

---

[1] Who summarizes and discusses its contents in his *Geschichte der gr.-röm. Philosophie*.

in some respect. But it is difficult to give concreteness to this general description of its nature (4^b 6–18). Since it is to be in some relation to the objects of sense whose primary characteristic is motion, it must be thought of as being the cause of motion, but evidently not through being moved itself. If it is to be thought of as causing motion without being moved, it must be thought to be an object of desire and thus to give rise to the rotation of the heavens (4^b 18–5^a 5).

Theophrastus evidently has before his mind the development of Greek metaphysical thought which in Plato drew the broad distinction between the sensible and the intelligible and described the intelligible as the cause of the sensible, and then in Aristotle refused to accept the Pythagorean-Platonic identification of the intelligible cause of the sensible world with mathematical objects and found it instead in an unmoved first mover operating as a final cause. And this account, he says, so far is sound. It assigns a single cause to all things, and assigns to this its activity and essence. And further it exhibits a regard for truth in not merely denying the first principle to be divisible but making it something non-quantitative (5^a 5–13).

So far Theophrastus indicates a preference for Aristotle's over Plato's metaphysics. But he is not merely expounding the Aristotelian system; he proceeds to criticize—at any rate to point out questions to which Aristotle furnishes no answer. If the mover is one, whence arises the fact that the heavenly bodies move in different directions; if there are more than one mover, how is harmony produced between the movements they initiate? (5^a 14–21). Further, the account given by the astronomers (and accepted by Aristotle in *Met.* 1073^b 11) of the number of the moving bodies is not adequate. And it is not clear why if these bodies are actuated by love for something unmovable they do not imitate it by being unmoved themselves (5^a 21–5). But in the middle of what seems clearly a criticism of Aristotle the writer inserts a sentence aimed at the Academic description of sensible things as imitating the

One or the numbers (5^a 25-8). It would seem that he is not following a very clear line of thought and that association of ideas has led him to pass from Aristotle's view that the heavenly bodies do their best to imitate the life of God, to the Platonic view that sensible things imitate the Ideas or the numbers. We shall see other instances of inconsecutiveness in Theophrastus' thought.

Returning to Aristotle, he urges that if the impulse of the heavenly bodies towards God is to be taken seriously they must be possessed of soul, and by that very fact have psychical movements of their own; thus even if the first cause produces their rotatory movement, it will not produce the best movement they have, which is their own psychical life, and in particular the movement of thought which is presupposed by their desire for the first cause (5^a 28–^{b} 10).

Further, he asks, why is impulse confined to the heavenly bodies and denied to the things of earth? It can hardly be supposed that the power of the first cause is not great enough to penetrate to them, and we must conclude that it is they that are unfit to receive it (5^b 10-18). Aristotle's account severs them from the heavenly bodies not only in position but in respect of their activity, in denying them rotation; and makes the movements and the mutual transformations of the elements the mere incidental result of the heavenly rotation (5^b 19-26).

Returning to the heavenly bodies, Theophrastus argues that we might expect them to receive from the first mover something better than rotary movement; for (and here again he seems to confuse Platonic with Aristotelian doctrine) the deity must be supposed to wish for the best for all things. Thus far Theophrastus seems to be following a monistic line of thought and criticizing Aristotle for the abrupt distinction he makes between the rotary movement of the heavenly spheres and the rectilinear movement of the terrestrial elements. He pulls himself up, however, with the reflection that it would be an exaggerated monism to say that all things must be exactly alike or admit of little difference (5^b 26–6^a 5). A question that may really be asked, however, is whether rotation is of the essence of the heavens, so that with its cessation they would perish, or is incidental to their possession of desire; and—even apart from the theory which explains their movement by desire—whether movement is essential or only incidental to them (6^a 5–15).

He passes to a broader criticism directed at the Platonic school. We may fairly demand that, whatever first principles a thinker adopts, he shall deduce the whole contents of the universe from them and not stop short after deducing only a few. In this respect (though perhaps ironically) Theophrastus singles out for praise the Pythagorean Eurytus, who not only said that numbers were the cause of things but was prepared to assign the number that constituted the essence of each animal species (6^a 15–22). Most members of the Pythagorean-Platonic school generate from their principles, the One and the indefinite dyad, only numbers, planes, and solids, from the indefinite dyad alone a few more entities, and from numbers and the One a few others again. Only Xenocrates, Hestiaeus, and Plato tried a more thoroughgoing account (6^a 23–^{b} 16). Some even identified reality with the first principles alone. In the other sciences the very opposite is the case; for in them stress is laid rather on what follows from the first principles. But perhaps (Theophrastus, as he often does, pulls himself up by recognizing the opposite half of the truth to that which he has been emphasizing) this difference is justified; metaphysics is after all a search for first principles, the other sciences are the deduction of conclusions from them (6^b 16–22).

Are the first principles to be conceived of as shapeless and merely potential or as already informed with shape and definite? It would seem that the first principles should be definite (as they are in the sciences and in the arts) and other things should derive definiteness from them. It would be absurd to hold that the universe and its parts are perfectly

INTRODUCTION xv

definite while its first principles are indefinite (6^b 23–7^a 19). At the same time it is difficult, on the hypothesis of definite first principles, to deduce from them a complete teleological explanation of animals, plants, and inanimate things; our best hope is to explain such phenomena by the movement of the heavenly bodies. But we must remember that it is a question how far definiteness (or law) extends in nature (7^a 19–^{b} 8).

We may also ask why the first principles should be supposed to be exempt from motion. If rest is better than motion it *should* be ascribed to the first principles; if it is a mere negation of motion we should ascribe to them not rest but activity (as distinct from motion) (7^b 9–15). So far the writer seems to be expressing a preference for Aristotle's first mover, which is described by Aristotle as activity, over Plato's static first principles, the One and the indefinite dyad. But he now turns to criticize Aristotle, and to suggest that the first cause may itself be in motion; i.e. to vindicate Plato's view of the soul as self-mover. We should not, he says, be afraid of the suggestion that at each stage in the causation of movement the mover may itself be in motion. Sense-perception confirms the view that mover and moved need not always be different (7^b 15–23). But he next turns to criticize a previous objection raised by himself (as well as by others) against Aristotle's system. It is a mistake, he says, to object that, though the heavenly bodies are actuated by desire for a first mover which is at rest, they do not imitate its freedom from movement. We must not treat the universe as if it were a simple entity without parts or differences; it is enough if the universe forms a harmonious whole which attains as much perfection as is possible for it (7^b 23–8^a 7). Again he seems to be protesting against a monism more thorough-going than the facts will warrant.

A further problem concerns the analysis of things into matter and form. Are we to think of matter as not existing but only potentially existing, or as existing but relatively indefinite, like the materials used by the arts, the essence of things that come into being depending on their possessing the opposite element of form? On this showing, while the acquisition of form is a change for the better, being is already present where there is matter—but indefinite and potential being (8^a 8–20).

Theophrastus next suggests a criticism of the Pythagorean view that the world is made up out of good and evil principles. A further question is why there is as much evil as good in the world. But this is like asking the improper question why all things are not alike. More paradoxical is the view that reality *cannot* exist without contraries, and still more paradoxical the view (apparently Democritus' theory of the void is meant) that that which neither is, was, nor will be must be counted in to the nature of the universe (8^a 21–^{b} 9).

It is clear, however, that there are different kinds of being. Sense-perception reveals differences between things and suggests to reason the task of explaining them. Knowledge therefore presupposes difference; and difference exists not only between universals, or between individuals falling under different universals, but between members of the same universal, whether this be a genus or a species (8^b 10–20). Practically everything that is known is peculiar to its possessor; this is true both of the substance of things and of their properties. It is the task of knowledge to detect identity in multiplicity, whether this identity is perfect or the common element takes a different form in its different manifestations. The end of knowledge is in some cases a universal; in others a particular, e.g. in dealing with objects of action and production (8^b 20–9^a 4). The identical something by which we know may be the same in essence or in number or in species or in genus or by analogy, but the greatest intervals are spanned by analogy (9^a 4–9).

Knowledge being of different kinds the essential thing is to follow the method appropriate to each class of object, i.e. one for intelligible objects and another for natural objects, and among the latter one for the simplest objects and another

INTRODUCTION xvii

for those that come later, such as animals and plants. There are different methods appropriate to different objects, as there are within mathematics (9^a 10-18). Parenthetically the author remarks that if some things are known in the sense that they are known to be unknown, still it is better to form some idea of them by the aid of analogy (9^a 18-23). The various kinds of knowledge can be distinguished only if we first have a general definition of knowledge, which is not easy. Nor is it easy to say up to what point one should push the search for causes; an infinite regress is at all events to be avoided. The writer accepts the Aristotelian view that there are 'first things' for which no cause is to be looked for, and which are apprehended by the direct 'contact' of thought (9^a 23–^{b} 16). It is a point of great importance and difficulty to know where to stop in our inquiries; it is clear that to demand a proof of everything is to make proof and knowledge impossible (9^b 16-24). But those who suppose the heavens to be eternal and accept the astronomical theories about the heavenly bodies have not come to the limits of knowledge; they have still to ask what are the first movers, and what is the final cause of the movement, and the essence and relations of the first movers, and to carry the explanation right down to animals and plants. There are higher entities in nature than those revealed by astronomy. The method of metaphysics is not, or not entirely, that of physics. Yet movement is of the essence of nature, and especially of the heaven, so that if deprived of movement it would be a heaven only in name. As life in animals needs no explanation or is to be explained as being their very essence, so is movement to be explained as the very essence of the heavenly system (9^b 24-10^a 21).

It is not easy to be certain that everything in nature has a final cause; many phenomena both celestial and terrestrial appear to be the result of coincidence or of mere necessity. What is the final cause of the movements of the sea, of droughts and moistures, of the transformation of things into one another? Animal life presents many phenomena that seem to be superfluous—the breasts of males, the growth of the beard, &c.; some features of animal life are positively unnatural (10^a 22–^{b} 16). Many facts about the nourishment and generation of animals seem to serve no final cause but to be the result of mechanical necessity. Again, plants and lifeless things present certain uniformities for which a final cause is hard to seek. It is not satisfactory to say these have no explanation, especially if we insist that in the *heavenly* region everything *is* explicable. It is plausible to say that these phenomena are simply the result of the rotation of the universe (10^b 16–11^a 1). We must, then, set limits to teleological explanation. We are told that nature everywhere desires the best, but if this be her desire it is clear that many things are recalcitrant to the good; there are fewer living things than lifeless, and of living things few whose existence is preferable to their non-existence. But to say that in the universe as a whole there is more positive evil (as distinct from mere indefiniteness) than good is a mistake. Rather the nature of reality is good (11^a 1–26).

Plato and the Pythagoreans make the distance between intelligible and sensible things a great one, but hold that the latter wish to imitate the former; yet they make an antithesis between the One and the indefinite dyad, and explain much by the latter, and hold that reality as a whole cannot dispense with it. Hence they must hold that God does not lead everything to the best, and could not even wish to do so if the abolition of one opposite meant the dissolution of reality (11^a 27–^{b} 12). Even among first things there is much that has no final cause and can only be explained as due to necessity. Among sensible things the heavenly bodies have most order; among intelligible things the objects of mathematics (11^b 12–23). It must be repeated that a limit should be recognized to final causation in the universe (11^b 24–12^a 2).

It will be seen that the arrangement of the work is not very good. Usener in his article *Zu Theophrast's metaphysischem Bruchstück* (*Rh. Mus.* 1861. 259-81)[1] suggested that various parts of the essay are not in their proper positions and that there are several lacunae. These views must be briefly examined.

(1) He holds that the objection to Aristotle's astronomical theory made in 5^b 26–6^a 5, that the πρῶτος οὐρανός might be expected to derive something better than rotation from the first mover, is connected in sense not with what immediately precedes, but with the argument in 5^a 28–^{b} 10, and is in fact a rather more theological treatment of the question which is there treated in the manner of physics. The next section, 6^a 5–15, follows, he holds, naturally after 5^b 26–6^a 5; and he therefore regards 5^b 10–26 as a note (by Theophrastus himself) which has wrongly been inserted in its present position. He points out, apparently as additional evidence of its being a mere note, that Theophrastus offers no solution to the question raised in it. But the same might be said of most of the questions raised in the work, which is aporematic throughout.

Theories of dislocation of the text should not be accepted except on very strong grounds, i.e. (apart from external evidence) only when (*a*) the existing order is improbably bad, and (*b*) the order produced by the rearrangement extremely good and natural. The first condition is not here fulfilled. It is true that 5^b 26–6^a 5 recurs to the question raised in 5^a 28–^{b} 10 with regard to the acquisition of rotation by the 'first heaven' from the first mover. But the intermediate passage follows quite naturally on the earlier passage, and there are two points of attachment between it and the later. There is the doubt as to rotation being the highest kind of activity, expressed in 5^b 21–3 and taken up ib. 26–8. And there is the suggestion that the things of earth do not share in rotation because they are ἄδεκτα (5^b 10–18), resumed in the suggestion that the first heaven does not get something better than rotation from the first mover because *it* is ἄδεκτον

---

[1] Reprinted in his *Kleine Schriften*, i. 91–111.

(ib. 26–6ª 1). The supposed dislocation may therefore be dismissed as improbable.

(2) Usener holds that in 6ª 15 the author turns from metaphysical discussions to a methodological one, which extends to ᵇ 22, the metaphysical inquiry being resumed in ch. 4. But 9ª 10–10ª 21 is also, he holds, methodological, and should come, and (he implies) originally did come, at the end of ch. 3.

On this distinction between 'metaphysical' and 'methodological' inquiries it may be remarked that, though Aristotle draws the distinction in theory, and holds that questions as to how a particular inquiry should be pursued and what may be expected from it should be settled before the inquiry itself is embarked upon, and though therefore Theophrastus was presumably familiar with the distinction, it is much harder to preserve it in practice than to recognize it in theory, and that even Aristotle is not very successful in doing so. In *Metaphysics* B, for example, of which the present treatise often reminds us, the first three (995ᵇ 4–13) and the fifth (ib. 18–27) of the questions proposed for discussion in ch. 1 are methodological; but between them comes the metaphysical question 'are there non-sensible as well as sensible substances?' (ib. 13–18). And every reader of the *Ethics* knows how the suggestions on method in that work come quite incidentally in the middle of the properly ethical discussion. Theophrastus, whose logical sense is weaker than Aristotle's, can hardly be expected to succeed in this respect, in which his master conspicuously failed. But further, 6ª 15–ᵇ 22 cannot in fact be said to be definitely methodological rather than metaphysical. It is not a formal discussion of method. It is a criticism of early philosophers for being content to explain a very few features of the universe by the aid of their first principles, and leaving the bulk of its phenomena unexplained. This criticism of them for failure to use their first principles belongs to the same line of thought as the preceding and following criticism of the first principles themselves. And this line of thought would in fact be seriously interrupted if we were to insert between 6ᵇ 22 and 23 the big stretch of really methodological inquiry concerning the kinds and the limits of knowledge, which we find in 9ᵃ 10–10ᵃ 21.

(3) Usener maintains that 8ᵇ 10–9ᵃ 9 (the discussion of the part played by difference in reality) is not in place where it is, and that it may have originally formed part of a discussion of the various kinds of knowledge which, according to one of Usener's alternative theories, has fallen out at 9ᵇ 24. He argues that at 9ᵇ 1 there has disappeared a passage in which the writer established the fact that knowledge is of causes, and that the writer could not *before* this passage have assumed, as he practically does in 8ᵇ 10–14, that knowledge is of causes.

Usener may be right in holding that there is a hiatus in 9ᵇ 1. For it is at first sight strange that, though Theophrastus has just propounded, without discussing, the question 'what is the nature of knowledge?' (9ᵃ 24–ᵇ 1), he should assume in ᵇ 2–3 that knowledge is essentially a search for causes. In his edition of the text (twenty-nine years later than the article we are discussing) Usener says nothing of the three rearrangements he there proposes, and he may have ceased to think them probable. But he still thinks it certain that a passage has disappeared at 9ᵇ 1 in which it was established that knowledge is of causes. This seems to us by no means certain. It seems more probable that Theophrastus did not accept, as a satisfactory answer to the question 'what is knowledge?', the statement 'knowledge is knowledge of causes', which is indeed no answer to the question since it uses in the definition the very term to be defined. We think rather that in ᵇ 2–3 he regards the view that knowledge is explanation by causes as an ἔνδοξον which itself needs discussion. The passage ᵇ 1–24 follows indeed very naturally after what precedes. For what immediately precedes is a statement of the difficulty of finding a common definition of a term which like 'knowledge' has different senses (^{a} 26-^{b} 1); and ^{b} 1-24 really develops this difficulty, for it points out that while knowledge of the facts of nature means explaining them by causes (^{b} 8-9), when we come to 'ultimates' this is impossible and we can only hope to apprehend without explaining them (^{b} 10-16). The writer is in fact drawing the distinction between ratiocinative knowledge and direct apprehension and failing to find anything common to them. And if so, he could hardly have already accepted as the answer to the question 'what is knowledge?' the dictum 'knowledge is explanation by causes'.

Further, 8^b 10-9^a 9 is naturally connected with what precedes it. For in 8^b 2-3 Theophrastus has remarked that, though we assert being of all things, we yet find them 'in no way like one another'; and 8^b 10-9^a 9 simply develops the notion that difference is an essential feature of the universe. And 8^b 10-9^a 9 is naturally followed by 9^a 10-^{b} 1; for in the earlier passage he develops the thesis that it is essential that knowledge should take account of the differences between things (8^b 16-24), and adds that in some subject-matters we can detect a numerical, in others a specific, in others a generic, in others only an analogical unity (9^a 4-9); and in the later passage he insists that the differences between its subject-matters impose difference on the method of knowledge itself (9^a 10-24).

(4) Usener, as we have seen, detects a gap at 9^b 24, and certainly the connexion between the passage beginning there and what precedes is not obvious. He has three alternative suggestions. (*a*) There may have dropped out from here a discussion of the question merely raised in ^{a} 23-4 'how many kinds of knowledge there are'; in which case 8^b 10-9^a 9 belongs here, since it is meant to lead up to an answer to that question. But we have seen that that section is in place where it is. (*b*) 9^b 24-10^a 21 may be meant merely to set aside the possible view that astronomy is the highest science, that which gives the most ultimate possible explana-

INTRODUCTION xxiii

tion of the universe, and forms the limit beyond which inquiry is fruitless; the notion that there is such a limit has already been put forward in 9^b 8-9. In that case, he thinks, not much has dropped out at 9^b 24—presumably merely a sentence linking the following section with 9^b 8-9. (*c*) In his edition he adopts a third view not very dissimilar from the second—that what has dropped out is a statement that (though there is a limit to explanation, 9^b 21-4) since science consists in explaining the nexus of causes, this study of causes must not be omitted; on this follows an illustration (9^b 24-10^a 5), viz. that astronomy must not rest content without an inquiry as to the first movers, and the final cause, of the heavenly movements. Alternatively, however, he suggests that there is no lacuna and that it may be enough to read τοῖς οὖν for ὅσοι in 9^b 24.

It seems to us that by simply inserting δέ after ὅσοι a good connexion of thought can be made out. There is a limit to explanation (9^b 21-4). But those who merely give us an astronomical theory of the celestial movements have not reached this limit. There remain the questions of the first movers and the final cause of movement. There are entities higher than those recognized by astronomy (9^b 24-10^a 7).

It appears, then, that none of the greater dislocations of the text or lacunae suggested by Usener is really established. The sequence of thought in the essay is not always very good, but there is no reason to suppose that we can improve it by rearrangements, for which, it must be remembered, there is no argument except supposed logical necessity.

Finally, Usener thinks that there is evidence of the conflation of two treatises by an early editor. χρόνον ... πλείω in 6^b 3-4, which Usener treats as a fragment from an alternative version, can well be explained otherwise (see note ad loc.). καὶ ... εἶναι in 7^a 15-19 Usener treats as part of an alternative version of the previous sentence. But when we consider the sentences carefully we see that their relation is this:—in 7^a 10-15 Theophrastus points out that it would admittedly be absurd to ascribe order to the details of the universe and none to its first principles; in 15-19 he adds the minor premiss 'yet this is just what those do who assert that the first principles are purely material'. Again, Usener treats ἔχει ... ἱκανῶς in 9ª 16-18 as a mere repetition of the previous sentence, but we give in our commentary an interpretation which seems to remove this objection. Once more, he treats Πλάτων ... ἀτόμων in 11ª 27-ᵇ 23 as a repetition of what precedes, but a glance at the two passages will show that they are substantially different, and that there is no difficulty in accepting them as parts of a single version.

On the other hand, ἢ ... μεθισταμένων in 10ᵇ 4-6 is an intolerable repetition of l. 3, and the μέν without any corresponding δέ indicates that it is a fragment of a longer alternative version. And it seems highly probable that in the same context ἢ τίνος αἱ προχωρήσεις ⟨καὶ ἀναχωρήσεις⟩, which seems to be a mere repetition of αἱ ἔφοδοι καὶ ἀνάρροιαι θαλάττης, comes from a duplicate version.

Thus we are left with two passages in one context, in which alternative versions are blended. It is unsafe to rest upon this the view that the work is a blending of two complete alternative versions; the facts would be quite explained by supposing that Theophrastus wrote alternative versions of this context, and that an editor rather unsuccessfully tried to work these into a single whole. That this editor was Tyrannio, as Usener thinks, is a reasonable conjecture, but we cannot put it higher than that.

There is no evidence that Theophrastus ever wrote a substantive work on metaphysics, nor does the present essay suggest that a metaphysical treatise by him, had he written one, would have been a very valuable work. The essay asks many interesting questions, but does not suggest that the author had any better answer to them than the earlier thinkers he criticizes. One of the main points of interest is the freedom of the writer from undue subservience to any of the schools of Greek philosophy. His standpoint is, in the main, that of an Aristotelian. But the sketch given above of the course of the work shows that he is capable of criticizing Aristotle's system and of selecting some of its weakest points for criticism, as for instance, the question of the relations between the first mover, the intelligences that move the planetary spheres, and the spheres themselves. In general it would be true to say that he expresses a distrust of premature system-building. We must not ascribe to the universe, he insists, more unity or a more teleological character than the facts will justify. But while this is a valuable warning, it does not amount to a constructive philosophical idea, and of such the essay shows no trace. In fact Theophrastus marks the culmination of the reaction which Aristotle began from the bold metaphysical speculations of Plato. Plato is a philosopher pure and simple; Aristotle is a man whose interest gradually turns from philosophical speculation to the study of detailed problems of natural science and history; Theophrastus is first and foremost a man of science. He has enough interest in metaphysics to ask intelligent questions, but there is nothing to suggest that he had either the interest or the ability that were needed to lead him to successful answers to his questions. Thus the value of the essay lies chiefly in the partial picture it gives us of the state of opinion in the Lyceum in the first generation after Aristotle, and in the few additional facts it gives us with regard to the philosophical systems earlier than Aristotle's.

Perhaps the most important positive suggestions Theophrastus has to make are (1) that there is no need to seek for an explanation of movement (as by an unmoved first mover), movement rather belonging to the very essence of the things that have it ($10^a 9-21$, cf. $6^a 5-14$); and (2) that many features of the universe are to be explained not teleologically but as the inevitable result of movements of the heavenly bodies ($7^a 22-^b 5$, $10^b 26-11^a 1$, $11^b 24-12^a 2$). But in the first of these suggestions he is anticipated by Plato and in the second by Aristotle. Both these suggestions har monize with the statements of Cicero (*De Deor. Nat.* I. 13. 35) and Clement of Alexandria (*Protr.* 5. 58, i. 51. 4-6 Stählin) that Theophrastus sometimes, at any rate, inclined to an identification of God with the celestial system. *Nec vero Theophrasti inconstantia ferenda est; modo enim menti divinum tribuit principatum, modo caelo, tum autem signis sideribusque caelestibus.* ὁ δὲ Ἐρέσιος ἐκεῖνος Θεόφραστος ὁ Ἀριστοτέλους γνώριμος πῇ μὲν οὐρανόν, πῇ δὲ πνεῦμα τὸν θεὸν ὑπονοεῖ.

The MSS. in which the essay is found are the following:—

J *Vindobonensis* phil. gr. C (olim 34), parchment (199 folia, mm. 280 × 192), saec. x ineuntis. This MS. has been described by A. Gercke, *Wiener Studien*, xiv (1892), 146-8; F. H. Fobes, *Classical Review*, xxvii (1913), 249, n. 3, and *Classical Philology*, x (1915), 189, n. 1. Early as it is, it contains, in the *Metaphysical Fragment*, one error that suggests a minuscule parent: 6ᵇ 12 δόξειεν ἄν] δόξει ἐρᾶν.

P *Parisinus*, Bibliothèque Nationale, Fonds grec 1853 (olim Mediceus Regius 2105), parchment (453 folia, mm. 350-53 × 245-60), saecc. x and xv. This MS. is the work of several hands; ff. 306ʳ-337ʳ, containing the present work, are probably by the fourth hand (saec. x)—by the second according to A. Förster, *Aristotelis De anima libri iii*, Budapestini, 1912, p. viii.

z *Parisinus*, Bibliothèque Nationale, Fonds grec 2277 (olim Mediceus Regius 3382 B), paper (134 folia, mm. 205 × 138), saec. xv-xvi.

A *Vaticanus* gr. 1302, paper (218 folia, mm. 326 × 237), saec. xiv.

V *Vaticanus* gr. 1305, vellum (207 folia, mm. 405 × 275), saec. xv (f. 20ᵛ: ἐγράφη διὰ χειρὸς ἐλαχίστου ἱερέως γεωργίου τοῦ τζαγγαροπούλου τοῦ κρητικοῦ + ἀμήν +).

O *Ottobonianus* gr. 153, paper (274 folia, mm. 220 × 164), saec. xv.

R *Palatinus* gr. 162, parchment (216 folia, mm. 277 × 198), saec. xv (the work of Iohannes Scutariota).

u *Reginensis* gr. 124, paper (369 folia, mm. 217 × 125), sacc. xvi.

Vᵃ *Urbinas* gr. 108, paper (151 folia, mm. 273 × 195), saec. xv.

L *Laurentianus* 28. 45 ('B' Brandis, Wimmer), paper (111 folia, mm. 193 × 142), anni 1445.
C *Marcianus* gr. 211, paper (281 folia, mm. 260 × 180), saec. xiii. According to Dr. Pesenti of the Marcian Library, the second hand—the hand of the scribe who wrote the section containing the present work—resembles the hand found in ff. 124 sqq. of Marcianus gr. 331, which certainly dates from saec. xiii.
M *Marcianus* gr. 260, paper (176 folia, mm. 210 × 140), saec. xiv.
D *Ambrosianus* P. 80 sup. (olim ⟨T⟩ 346), parchment (64 folia, mm. 245 × 169), saec. xv.
B *Bernensis*, Bibliothèque de la Ville 402, paper (ii + 139 folia, mm. 234 × 152), saec. xv.
H *Vossianus* gr. 4º. 25, paper (163 folia, mm. 230 × 155), saec. xv.
S *Londiniensis*, British Museum Add. 5113, paper (73 folia, mm. 235 × 165), saec. xv.

For the readings of L the editors have had the advantage of a very careful collation kindly made for them by Professor Rostagno, to whom they take this occasion to express their warmest thanks. B has been collated from photographs; the other fourteen MSS. from rotographs. Certain readings in the Vatican MSS. and in P have been verified by Mr. Ross from the MSS. themselves. For miscellaneous information about the MSS. the editors wish to acknowledge their indebtedness to the courteous assistance of Dr. Omont of the National Library in Paris, Monsignore Mercati of the Vatican Library, Dr. Ferrari and Dr. Pesenti of the Marcian Library, Dr. Gramatica of the Ambrosian Library, Dr. Thormann of the City Library in Berne, and Dr. Büchner of the University Library in Leyden. The collation of the *editio princeps* has been made from the magnificent copy in the library of Professor Herbert Weir Smyth, to whom also the editors express their thanks.

The archetype contained the following errors, if the text presented in this book is correct: $4^b 2$ ἔχει; ὥστε; $5^a 23$ ἀρκεῖ om.; $^b 2$ διαφοράν; 6–7 ἔμψυχοι; 18 ἀσύνθετον; 23 συμβαίνει; $7^a 9$ ὄν om.; 14 σάρξ; 15 ὁ; $^b 16$ ἀεὶ κινοῦν; 20 δεῖ; $8^a 2$ εἰ;

οὖσιν ἀκολουθείη ; 9ª 1 ἔνια τῶν ; 7 ἀπέχοντες ; 14 τὰ om. ; b 20 περί τε ; 24 δὲ om. ; 10ª 11 ἤ ; 17 τε ; 23 θ' om. ; b 1 ἢ τίνος αἱ προχωρήσεις ; 4–6 ἢ . . . μεθισταμένων ; 12 οὐκ ὠφελουμένοις, τοῖς om. ; 13 κινήσει ; 11ª 5 εἰκὸς om. ; 18 ἀκαριαῖον ; 20 ἤ ; ἐν] εἰ ; b 12 ἐν om. ; 18 τε.

That the MSS. fall into two families is shown by the following passages, in which P alone is right, the fifteen other MSS. agreeing in error : 7ᵇ 12 τις] P : τῆς ceteri ; 18 λογῶδες] P : λογωειδες J : λογοειδὲς ceteri ; 8ᵇ 12 ὑποβάλλει] P : ὑπερβάλλει JLCVªOBHSz AD : ὑπερβάλλον MVR : ὑπερβάλλοντα u ; 27 τέλεος δ' ἡ] τελεος δ' ἡ P : τέλος δ' Vⁿ O z : τέλος δὲ ceteri ; 10ª 1 τά τε] τατε P : τὰ δὲ JLC : ταῦτα δὲ M₁z : αὐτὰ δὲ τὰ u : ταῦτα δὲ τὰ M corr. ceteri ; 11ᵇ 5 ὅλως] ὅλως P : ὅλως δὲ BHS : ὅλως δ' ceteri.

The interrelations of the other MSS. are shown in the following paragraphs.

JLC. 4ª 21 παντός] τοῦ παντὸς JLC ; 7ᵇ 3 ἐτησίους] corr. Usener : ἐστησίους P : αἰτίους JLC : ἐτείους ceteri ; 10ª 1 τά τε] τατε P : τὰ δὲ JLC : ταῦτα δὲ M₁z : αὐτὰ δὲ τὰ u : ταῦτα δὲ τὰ M corr. ceteri ; 11ª 1 του om. JLC.

VªOMVRBHSu z AD. 4ª 16 τῶν φθαρτῶν] PJ corr. LC : τῶν ἀφθάρτων J₁ : τοῖς φθαρτοῖς ceteri ; 5ª 24 ὄρεξιν] PJLC : ἕξιν BSD : ἔξιν ceteri ; ᵇ 26 τὸ ἄριστον ἀπὸ τοῦ] PJLCH rec. : spatio relicto omittunt ceteri ; 6ª 19 ὅ περ] JLC : ὅπερ P : ὅπως ceteri.

LC form the most clearly defined of the sub-groups, in spite of the fact that they both have numerous individual errors ; L has more individual errors than any other MS. except u. 4ª 10 κοινωνία (κινωνία S) πρὸς ἄλληλα] π. ἀ. κ. LC ; ᵇ 3 ἐμποιῆσαι] ἐν ποιῆσαι L : ἐν ποιῆ C ; ζωὴν καὶ κίνησιν] ζωὴ καὶ κίνησις LC ; 19 τῆς om. LC (homoeotel.) ; 6ª 6 ἴσως ἀπορήσειε(ν)] ἀ. ἴ. LC ; 21 λέγειν] λέγει LC ; 8ª 18 ποιόν] τὸ ποιὸν LC ; 9ᵇ 1 πλεοναχῶς] πολλαχῶς LC ; 15 καὶ pr. om. LC ; 17 ἡ alt. om. LC. LC twice share error due apparently to some abbreviation for ἄρα : 8ᵇ 16 ἄρα] ἔστιν LC ; 9ᵇ 6 εἰ ἄρα] ἔτι L : εἰ ἔστι C. At 10ᵇ 27 L has likewise ἔστι for ἄρα, though C has preserved the correct reading in the abbreviation (with breathing and accent) mentioned by Lehmann,[1] pp. 89-90.

---

[1] O. Lehmann. *Die tachygraphischen Abkürzungen der griechischen Handschriften.* Leipzig, 1880.

INTRODUCTION xxix

VaO. 4ᵇ 18 ἢ πειστικωτέρως om. VaO (homoeotel.); 5ᵃ 28 εἰ δ' ἡ] εἰ δὴ J₁LCMVAcorr.: ἐν δὴ VaO: ἐδὴ R z A₁D: ἔδη BHS: ἤδη u; 8ᵃ 15 οὐθὲν] οὐθὲν P: αθὲν (spatio antecedente) VaO: ἀθὲν R₁B₁HS z AD; 11ᵃ 21 τὰ] τοῦ VnO.

MVRBHS u. 5ᵃ 16 ὑπεναντίαι] ὑπεναντίον MVR: ὑπεναντίων B₁HS u: ὑπέναντι z; 10ᵃ 23 ἀφορισμὸς] ἀφωρισμὸς MVRBH z Dcorr.

AD. 4ᵇ 12 κατ' ἀναλογίαν εἴ τε iterant AD (homoeotel.); 8ᵃ 19 ἀναλογίαν] ἀνολογίαν AD: ἀναγίαν z₁: ἀνογίαν corr. z. Since D has no individual errors, the readings of A are not reported in our critical apparatus.

MVR. 5ᵇ 28 κυκλοφορίας] κυκλοφωρίας MVR; 6ᵃ 22 ἄλλου τινὸς] ἀλλ' οὔ τινος MV: ἀλλ' οὔ τινος R: ἀλού τινος z; 7ᵇ 11 ἀνάψειεν ἄν] ἀνάψει ἐν J₁ (ut vid.) u: ἀνάψιεν ἂν MVR; 8ᵇ 15 φωτὶ ζητούντων; φωτὶ ζητοῦντων S₁A: φωτίζητούντων B z D: φωτίζητούτων MVR; 10ᵇ 14 δή] δεῖ J: δ' ἡ MR: δ ἡ V.

BHS u. 7ᵇ 19 τρόπον] πρότερον BHS u; 8ᵃ 25 πολλῷ] πολλὼ P: πολὺ BHS u; ᵇ 26 ἀριθμοῖς] ἀριθμοῦ BHS u; 10ᵃ 7 τὰ] γὰρ τὰ L: δὲ BHS u; 11ᵃ 21 ἀμαθεστάτου] ἀμαθέστατον BHS u.

BHS. 4ᵃ 3 πρώτων] τρόπων B₁HS; 5ᵃ 28 εἰ δ' ἡ] εἰ δὴ J₁LCMVAcorr.: ἐν δὴ VaO: ἐδὴ R z A₁D: ἔδη BHS: ἤδη u; 8ᵃ 16 ὑπάρχοι] ὑπάρχει LCVᵃMVR z D: ὑπάρχῃ O: ὑπάρχων B₁HS: ὑπάρχον corr. B: ὑπάρχειν u.

BH. 8ᵇ 14 ἐνεργαζομένῃ] ἐνεργαζομένηι J: ἐργαζομένῃ LCVᵃ OMVRBcorr. S u z AD: ἐργαζομένην B₁H; 24 πλείοσιν] πλείωσιν P: πείοσι B₁H.

The resulting stemma is depicted in Figure 1 on p. xxx.

Three passages which appear to make against this stemma require special mention: 9ᵃ 6 διαιρέσεις] διαιρέσει PJL: διαίρεσις (perhaps the true reading) COVS; 23 ἀόρατον] ὁρατόν PJLC; 10ᵇ 12 λελωβημένοις] λελωβημένων PJLC. The first two passages can be readily explained either by supposing independent agreement in error by P and γ (to the cursory reader διαιρέσει and ὁρατόν are probably *lectiones faciliores*) or by supposing that the error found in P and in γ goes back to the archetype and that the presence of the correct reading in δ is due to emendation, easy in the first passage, less easy in the second. In the third passage the archetype, after the loss of οὐκ ὠφελουμένοις, τοῖς by haplography, had embodied the attempted correction λελωβημένων to agree with ἐλάφων; δ then, dissatisfied with this, altered to λελωβημένοις to agree with τοῖς, and thus hit by accident on part of the true reading.

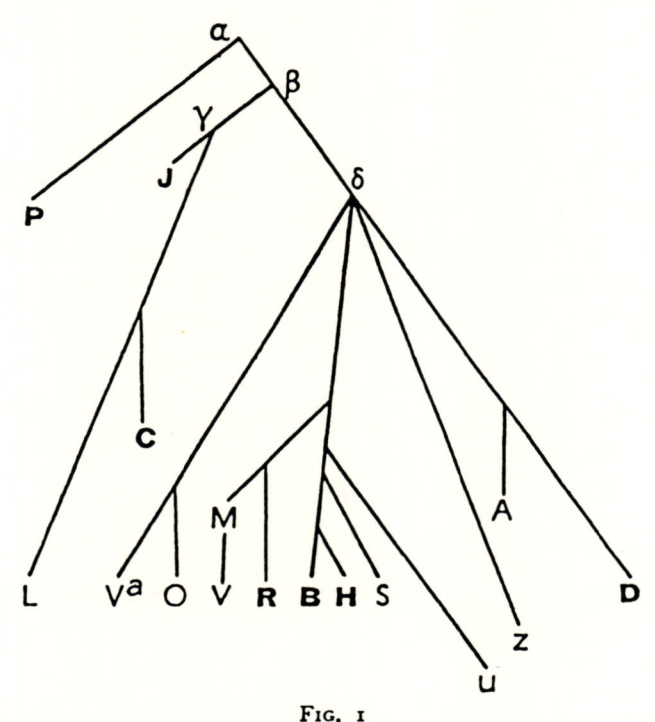

FIG. 1

The MSS. whose readings are reported in the critical apparatus are indicated by bold-face capitals.

There is contamination between C and V^aO : 5^b 13 οὐ om. L,CV^aO ; 7^a 22 φυτοῖς] ἐν φυτοῖς CV^aO u; 11^a 22 εἰκῇ γάρ] corr. Sylburg : ει· καὶ γὰρ P : καὶ γὰρ J : καὶ L : εἰ γὰρ καὶ CV^aO : εἰ καὶ γὰρ ceteri. In spite of the fact that both L and C are suspect on other grounds (7^a 19 δ' om. JL ; ^b 20 μὴ ἀεί] corr. Wimmer : μὴ δεῖ PJz : καὶ ὡς δεῖ L : μὴ δὴ ceteri ; 8^a 23 ἐν] ἢ L : om. CV^aOMVRBH u AD ; 9^a 6 διαιρέσεις] διαιρέσει PJL : διαίρεσις COVS ; ^b 2 γε] PJ : τε ceteri ; 14 τῶν τοιούτων] PJ : om. ceteri ; 10^a 23 ἄλλως θ'] corr. Usener : αλλως P : ἄλλως JL : ἀλλ' ὡς ceteri ; 11^a 4 διστασμὸν] PL : δυσταγμὸν J : διστάγμὸν C₁ ceteri ; λεγόμενα] PJLO : λέγομεν ἃ ceteri), it has seemed best, since δ (*vid. supra*, Figure 1) is abundantly represented by other MSS. than V^aO and since the individual errors of L are very numerous, to disregard both L and V^aO and to record the readings of C.

Contamination between L and M is suggested by 4^b 21 ταύτην τῆς κινήσεως] ταύτης τῆς κινήσεως LCMV; 6^a 5 τόδε] τοτε L: τό τε MV; and is confirmed by 8^a 15 οὐθέν] οὐθὲν P: αθὲν (spatio antecedente) V^aO: ἀθὲν R₁B₁HS z AD. The last case shows that the fault lies with M, not with L. Not infrequently L agrees with a correction of J: 6^a 26, ^b 3-4, 12, 7^a 7, ^b 1, 17, 8^a 2.

V is probably a direct descendant of M (which has no individual error except at 7^a 5): 7^a 5 αἴ περ] αἴπερ P: ὥπερ M₁: ὥσπερ V; 9^h 14 τῷ om. MV (homoeotel.); 11^a 6 ἀρίστου] ἀορίστου MV; ^b 18 αἰσθητῶν] ἀθλητῶν MV. Among its numerous individual errors are three dittographies, all of which are explicable by homoeoteleuton and only one of which (4^a 20, where, after writing αἰσθητοῖς, the scribe went back to μαθηματικοῖς (18)) is of such a length that the error would have been facilitated by the length of M's lines. V shares trivial errors with several other MSS.: JC (8^b 7 γεγονὸς] γεγονὼς J₁V₁: γεγονῶς C₁), L (5^b 12 τὸ] τῶν L₁V), COS (9^a 6 διαιρέσεις] διαιρέσει PJL: διαίρεσις COVS), O (10^b 2 ἀναξηράνσεις] ἀναξηράσεις O₁V), Su (10^a 19 ἀφωρισμένον] ἀφορισμένον V₁Su). Whether or not these last errors result from contamination, V is worthless.

S shares trivial errors with several MSS. other than BH: J (9^b 13 φωτεινότατα] φωτινότατα JS: ποθεινόμτα A₁: ποθεινότατα V^aOMVRB₁H u z A corr. D), L (9^a 13 τε] δὲ), V, u (10^a 19 ἀφωρισμένον] ἀφορισμένον), H (7^b 6 ἀφορισμὸν] ἀφωρισμὸν V^aMRBz AD: ἀφωσισμὸν HS: ἀφοσιασμὸν u; 9^a 20 ἴδιος] εἴδιος H₁S), z (7^b 13 ἀντιμεταλλακτέον] τι μεταλλακτέον PJL corr. C corr. A: τι μεταλακτέον L₁: τὴν μεταλλακτέον C₁: ἀντιμεταλακτέον Sz). Of all these instances 7^b 6 (agreement with H) is perhaps the least likely to have resulted from independent error; and since B and H, which are above suspicion and are comparatively free from individual errors, have been seen to stand together against S, it has seemed best to disregard S entirely.

u shares one serious error and several trivial errors with MSS. other than BHS: J (5^b 1 ἀρίστου] ἀορίστου J₁ u; 10^a 25 τῷ] τῶν), CV^{a}O (7^a 22 φυτοῖς] ἐν φυτοῖς), O$_1$ (5^b 4 αἱ ὀρέξεις] ὄρεξις), MVR (8^b 12 ὑποβάλλει] ὑπερβάλλει JLCV^{a}OBHS z AD : ὑπερβάλλον MVR : ὑπερβάλλοντα u), V$_1$S (10^a 19 ἀφωρισμένον] ἀφορισμένον). Because of the suspicion of contamination which these errors provoke and because of the large number of individual errors (over sixty—more than in any other MS.), it has seemed best to disregard the MS. altogether. A MS. closely related to u was apparently the chief source of the *editio princeps* and so of Oporinus. The *editio princeps* agrees with u in occasional wrong accents and wrong breathings and in two nonsensical readings (9^a 4 αὐτῶν] ἂν τῶν ; 10^b 3 ἄλλοτ'] ἄλλο τ'), but most of u's minor errors it does not share ; nor does it share four of u's omissions (5^a 22 τῆς, 6^a 16 καὶ, 8^b 4 δὲ, 9^a 18 καὶ); but its only other serious divergence from u is 7^a 22 φυτοῖς] *ed. pr.* : ἐν φυτοῖς CV^{a}O u.

z shows slight traces of contamination from several sources : 6^a 21 ὁ om. O z ; 7^b 13 ἀντιμεταλλακτέον] τι μεταλλακτέον PJ L corr. C corr. A : τι μεταλακτέον L$_1$: τὴν μεταλλακτέον C$_1$: ἀντιμεταλακτέον S z ; 20 μὴ ἀεὶ] corr. Wimmer : μὴ δεῖ PJ z : καὶ ὡς δεῖ L : μὴ δὴ ceteri ; 8^a 15 μετάβασις] μετάβασι z D ; 10^a 1 τά τε] τατε P : τὰ δὲ JLC : ταῦτα δὲ M$_1$ z : αὐτὰ δὲ τὰ u : ταῦτα δὲ τὰ M corr. ceteri.

In the matter of orthography there is little to remark. ἅμα in J nowhere has ι, whereas in P it has it everywhere except at 9^b 22. γίνομαι nowhere has a second γ in either P or J. οὐθείς and μηθείς are spelt with θ in P and J except at 10^a 22, where both P and J have δ. P admits hiatus less frequently than does J ; in no passage where P admits hiatus does J elide. ν paragogicum before consonants is much more frequent in P than in J ; wherever it occurs in J it occurs also in P. All the MSS. have πλεῖον at 11^a 16 and πλέον elsewhere. In all these details we have followed P.

We have printed Usener's page- and line-numbers in the inner margin, and our references are to them.

SIGLA

P = Parisinus gr. 1853, saec. x
J = Vindobonensis phil. gr. C, saec. x ineuntis
C = Marcianus gr. 211, saec. xiii
R = Palatinus gr. 162, saec. xv ⎫
B = Bernensis 402, saec. xv ⎪
H = Vossianus gr. 4°. 25, saec. xv ⎬ Σ
D = Ambrosianus P. 80 sup., saec. xv ⎭
codd. = codicum PJCRBHD consensus
cet. = codicum PJCRBHD ceteri

      Raro citantur

L ('B' Brandis, Wimmer) = Laurentianus 28. 45, saec. xv
V^a = Urbinas gr. 108, saec. xv
O = Ottobonianus gr. 153, saec. xv
M = Marcianus gr. 260, saec. xiv
V = Vaticanus gr. 1305, saec. xv
S = Londiniensis Add. 5113, saec. xv
u = Reginensis gr. 124, saec. xvi
z = Parisinus gr. 2277, saecc. xv-xvi
A = Vaticanus gr. 1302, saec. xiv
interpres = Versionis latinae auctor (Cardinalis Bessario, si recte Fabricius-Harles) primum anno 1515 Parisiis ab H. Stephano editae. Hac nos usi sumus qualem exhibet editio Iuntina prima (Aristotelis ... Opera ... Io. Baptistae Bagolini labore ... Venetiis, 1550-53, vol. viii)

ΘΕΟΦΡΑΣΤΟΥ ΤΩΝ ΜΕΤΑ ΤΑ ΦΥΣΙΚΑ 4ᵃ

p. 308. 309 Brandisii

I 1   Πῶς ἀφορίσαι δεῖ καὶ ποίοις τὴν ὑπὲρ τῶν πρώτων θεωρίαν; ἡ γὰρ δὴ τῆς φύσεως πολυχουστέρα, καὶ ὥς γε δή τινές φασιν, ἀτακτοτέρα, μεταβολὰς ἔχουσα παντοίας· ἡ δὲ τῶν πρώτων ὡρισμένη καὶ ἀεὶ κατὰ ταὐτά· διὸ δὴ καὶ ἐν νοητοῖς, οὐκ αἰσθητοῖς, αὐτὴν τιθέασιν ὡς ἀκινήτοις καὶ ἀμεταβλήτοις, καὶ τὸ ὅλον δὲ σεμνοτέραν καὶ 2 μείζω νομίζουσιν αὐτήν. Ἀρχὴ δέ, πότερα συναφή τις καὶ οἷον κοινωνία πρὸς ἄλληλα τοῖς τε νοητοῖς καὶ τοῖς τῆς φύσεως, ἢ οὐδεμία ἀλλ' ὥσπερ ἑκάτερα κεχωρισμένα συνεργοῦντα δέ πως εἰς τὴν πᾶσαν οὐσίαν. εὐλογώτερον δ' οὖν εἶναί τινα συναφὴν καὶ μὴ ἐπεισοδιῶδες τὸ πᾶν, ἀλλ' οἷον τὰ μὲν πρότερα τὰ δ' ὕστερα, καὶ ἀρχὰς τὰ δ' ὑπὸ τὰς ἀρχάς, ὥσπερ καὶ τὰ ἀΐδια τῶν φθαρτῶν. εἰ δ' οὖν οὕτω, τίς ἡ φύσις αὐτῶν καὶ ἐν 3 ποίοις; εἰ μὲν γὰρ ἐν τοῖς μαθηματικοῖς μόνον τὰ νοητά, καθά περ | τινές φασιν, οὔτ' ἄγαν εὔσημος ἡ συναφὴ τοῖς αἰσθητοῖς, οὔθ' ὅλως ἀξιόχρεα φαίνεται παντός· οἷον γὰρ μεμηχανημένα δοκεῖ δι' ἡμῶν εἶναι σχήματά τε καὶ μορφὰς καὶ

4ᵃ 1 τῶν om. CO   τὰ om. P u   2 Ὡς Σ (deest in codicis D margine littera Ω maiuscula)   3 πρώτων marg. B: τρόπων B₁H πολυχιδεστέρα (-ιδε- ex corr.) C: πολυχεστέρα RBH corr. D: πολυσχεστέρα H₁: πολυσχιδεστέρα u   4 καὶ] ἢ Σ   5 μεταβολὴν ἔχουσα παντοίαν (-αν ex corr.) C   6 ταυτα P: ταῦτα JC₁: τὰ αὐτὰ Σ   9 ποτέρα J₁Σ: πότερόν ἐστιν J rec.: προτέρα C   10 πρὸς ἄλληλα κοινωνία C   12 κεχωρισμένα ἑκάτερα ci. Usener   13 δ' om. Σ

TRANSLATION

How, and by what distinguishing marks, should we delimit the study of first principles? The study of *nature* is more multifarious in its scope, and, as some at least maintain, more unorderly in its nature, comprising as it does all manner of changes; the study of first principles is definite and unchanging; which is the reason also why men describe it as concerned with objects of reason, not of sense, on the ground that these are unmovable and unchangeable, and why in general, too, they think it a more dignified and greater study.

Our starting-point is the question whether there is a connexion and as it were a mutual partnership between objects of reason and the things of nature, or there is none, but the two are, so to speak, separated, though they co-operate somehow to make up the whole of reality. It is, at all events, more reasonable to suppose that there is a connexion and that the universe is not a mere series of episodes, but some things are, so to speak, prior and others posterior—some, ruling principles, and others, subordinate to them—as eternal things are prior to and ruling principles of those that are perishable. If this *is* so, what is their nature and in what sort of things are they found? (1) If the objects of reason are found in mathematical objects only, as some say, neither is their connexion with objects of sense very conspicuous, nor do they appear, in general, equal to their whole task; for (*a*) they seem to have been, as it were, devised by us in the act of investing

---

14 ἐπισωδιῶδες J₁: ἐπισωδιῶδες εἶναι J rec.   15 καί] καὶ τὰ μέν J rec.   16 τῶν ἀφθάρτων J₁: τοῖς φθαρτοῖς Σ   18 μόνοις Σ   20 ἀξιοχρέα JRB₁HD   21 παντός] τοῦ παντὸς JC   22 δι'] δ' Σ

ΘΕΟΦΡΑΣΤΟΥ

p. 309 Brandisii

λόγους περιτιθέντων, αὐτὰ δὲ δι᾽ αὑτῶν οὐδεμίαν ἔχειν φύσιν· εἰ δὲ μή, οὐχ οὕτως γε συνάπτειν τοῖς τῆς φύσεως ὥστ᾽ ἐμποιῆσαι καθά περ ζωὴν καὶ κίνησιν αὐτοῖς· οὐδὲ γὰρ αὐτὸς ὁ ἀριθμός, ὅν περ δὴ πρῶτον καὶ κυριώτατόν τινες τιθέασιν. 4 εἰ δ᾽ ἑτέρα τις οὐσία προτέρα καὶ κρείττων ἐστίν, ταύτην πειρατέον λέγειν, πότερον μία τις κατ᾽ ἀριθμὸν ἢ κατ᾽ εἶδος ἢ κατὰ γένος. εὐλογώτερον δ᾽ οὖν ἀρχῆς φύσιν ἐχούσας ἐν ὀλίγοις εἶναι καὶ περιττοῖς, εἰ μὴ ἄρα καὶ πρώτοις καὶ ἐν τῷ πρώτῳ. τίς δ᾽ οὖν αὕτη καὶ τίνες, εἰ πλείους, πειρατέον ἐμφαίνειν ἀμῶς γέ πως εἴτε κατ᾽ ἀναλογίαν εἴτε κατ᾽ ἄλλην ὁμοίωσιν. ἀνάγκη δ᾽ ἴσως δυνάμει τινὶ καὶ ὑπεροχῇ τῶν ἄλλων λαμβάνειν, ὥσπερ ἂν εἰ τὸν θεόν· θεία γὰρ ἡ πάντων ἀρχή, δι᾽ ἧς ἅπαντα καὶ ἔστιν καὶ διαμένει. τάχα μὲν οὖν ῥᾴδιον τὸ οὕτως ἀποδοῦναι, χαλεπὸν δὲ σαφεστέρως ἢ πειστικωτέρως. 5 Τοιαύτης δ᾽ οὔσης τῆς ἀρχῆς, ἐπεί περ συνάπτει τοῖς αἰσθητοῖς, ἡ δὲ φύσις ὡς ἁπλῶς εἰπεῖν ἐν κινήσει καὶ τοῦτ᾽ αὐτῆς τὸ ἴδιον, δῆλον ὡς αἰτίαν θετέον ταύτην τῆς κινήσεως· ἐπεὶ δ᾽ ἀκίνητος καθ᾽ αὑτήν, φανερὸν ὡς οὐκ ἂν εἴη τῷ κινεῖσθαι τοῖς τῆς φύ-

4ᵃ 23 περιτεθέντων J₁CΣ   αὐτῶν P : αὑτῶν cet.
4ᵇ 2 ἔχειν corr. B : ἔχει P : ἔχει cet.   οὐχ οὕτως γε corr. Usener : οὐχ᾽ ὥστε P : οὐχ ὥστε JH : οὐχ᾽ ὥστε cet.   3 ὥστε ἐν ποιῆσαι (ὥστε ἐν ποιῇ C) καθάπερ ζωῇ καὶ κίνησις LC   6 εἰ] ἡ Σ   9 οὖν (οὐσίαν) Usener   ἔχουσαν Σ   9 εἶναι καὶ] εἰ ἦν RB₁HD : εἰ ἐν marg. B   11 εἰ P : οἱ Σ   12 κατ᾽ ἀναλογίαν εἴτε iterat D   18 ἡ (ἢ PJ) πιστικωτέρως PJC   19 τῆς om. LC   21 ταύτην] ταύτης C

things with figures and shapes and ratios, and to have no nature in and of themselves; and (*b*) if this is not so, at least they seem not to connect with the things of nature in such a way as to produce in them, as it were, life and motion; for not even number itself does so, which some in fact rank as the first and most dominant of all things. But (2) if there is 4 another reality prior and superior to the objects of mathematics, we ought to try to specify this and say whether it is a single reality in number or in species or in genus. It is, at all events, more reasonable to suppose that, having the nature of a ruling principle, they should be found only in a few things and things of no ordinary kind, if not, indeed, only in things that are primary, and in the first of all things. What, at any rate, this reality is, or what these realities are, if they are more than one, we must try to indicate somehow or other, whether in virtue of an analogy or of some other comparison. It is necessary, presumably, to recognize them by some power and some superiority to other things, as if it were God that we were apprehending; for the ruling principle of all things, through which all things both are and endure, *is* divine. Now it is, perhaps, easy to describe them thus, but difficult to do so more clearly or more convincingly.

Such being the ruling principle, since it connects 5 with sensible things and nature is, broadly speaking, in movement and this is its special property, it is clear that the ruling principle must be ranked as a cause of movement; but since it is in itself unmovable, it is evident that it could not be by being moved that it serves as cause to the things of nature, and the only alternative is that it should be by some

p. 309. 310 Brandisii

σεως αἰτία, ἀλλὰ λοιπὸν ἄλλῃ τινὶ δυνάμει κρείτ- 5ᵃ
τονι καὶ προτέρᾳ· τοιαύτη δ' ἡ τοῦ ὀρεκτοῦ φύσις, ἀφ' ἧς ἡ κυκλικὴ ἡ συνεχὴς καὶ ἄπαυ-
στος. | ὥστε κατ' ἐκεῖνο λύοιτο ἂν τὸ μὴ εἶναι
6 κινήσεως ἀρχὴν ἢ εἰ κινούμενον κινήσει. Μέχρι 5
μὲν δὴ τούτων οἷον ἄρτιος ὁ λόγος, ἀρχήν τε
ποιῶν μίαν πάντων καὶ τὴν ἐνέργειαν καὶ τὴν
οὐσίαν ἀποδιδούς, ἔτι δὲ μὴ διαιρετὸν μηδὲ ποσόν
τι λέγων ἀλλ' ἁπλῶς ἐξαίρων εἰς κρείττω τινὰ
μερίδα καὶ θειοτέραν· οὕτω γὰρ μᾶλλον ἀποδο- 10
τέον ἢ τὸ διαιρετὸν καὶ μεριστὸν ἀφαιρετέον.
ἅμα γὰρ ἐν ὑψηλοτέρῳ τε καὶ ἀληθινωτέρῳ λόγῳ
τοῖς λέγουσιν ἡ ἀπόφασις.

II 7 Τὸ δὲ μετὰ ταῦτ' ἤδη λόγου δεῖται πλείονος
περὶ τῆς ἐφέσεως, ποία καὶ τίνων, ἐπειδὴ πλείω 15
τὰ κυκλικὰ καὶ αἱ φοραὶ τρόπον τινὰ ὑπεναντίαι,
καὶ τὸ ἀνήνυτον καὶ οὗ χάριν ἀφανές. εἴτε γὰρ
ἓν τὸ κινοῦν, ἄτοπον τὸ μὴ πάντα τὴν αὐτήν·
εἴτε καθ' ἕκαστον ἕτερον αἵ τ' ἀρχαὶ πλείους,
ὥστε τὸ σύμφωνον αὐτῶν εἰς ὄρεξιν ἰόντων τὴν 20
8 ἀρίστην οὐθαμῶς φανερόν. τὸ δὲ κατὰ τὸ πλῆθος τῶν σφαιρῶν τῆς αἰτίας μείζονα ζητεῖ λόγον·
οὐ γὰρ ⟨ἀρκεῖ⟩ ὅ γε τῶν ἀστρολόγων. ἄπορον δὲ
καὶ πῶς ποτε φυσικὴν ὄρεξιν ἐχόντων οὐ τὴν ἠρε-

5ᵃ 1 δυνάμει] sequitur in J rasura unius litt.   κρεῖττον J₁   3 κυκλικὴ ⟨κίνησις⟩ Usener   ἄπαυτος P : ἄπαυστος C   4 κατ' ἐκεῖνο] κἀκεῖνο ci. Camotius : καὶ ἐκεῖνο Usener   5 εἰ in J eras.   κινήσει] φύσει B₁   12 τε om. BH u   15 ποῖα PJ   16 ὑπεναντίον R : ὑπεναντίων B₁H u   19 αἵ τ'] ἔτ' (ut vid.) J   20 τὸ om. u   ὄντων C : ἰόντων B₁H corr.   23 ἀρκεῖ inserendum ci. Usener   ἀστρολόγων] ἀστρολόγων ἱκανὸς J rec : an ἀστρολόγων ⟨ἀξιόλογον⟩?   24 ὄρεξιν] ἕξιν RH : ἕξιν BD

other power superior and prior to this; and such is the nature of the object of desire, from which proceeds the circular movement which is continuous and unceasing. Thus in the object of desire we should find the solution of the objection that the only possible source of movement is one which will move by being moved.

So far, then, the account fits, so to speak, well together, both in setting up one ruling principle of all things and in assigning its activity and essence; and further in not describing it as something divisible or quantitative, but raising it absolutely into a better and more divine region; for this is the account we ought to give, rather than merely remove from it liability to division and partition. For this complete denial involves, for those who make it, an account that is at the same time more lofty and rings truer.

The next problem already demands more discussion, viz. the problem about the impulse in question, what manner of impulse it is and towards what objects; since the rotating bodies are more than one and their motions are in some sense opposed, and the fact that their motion is never finished, and the end to which it is directed, are obscure. For (1) if that which imparts movement is one, it is strange that it does not move all the bodies with the same motion; and (2) if that which imparts movement is different for each moving body and the sources of movement are more than one, then their 'harmony as they move in the direction of the best desire' is by no means obvious. And the matter of the number of the spheres demands a fuller discussion of the reason for it; for the *astronomers'* account is not adequate. It is hard to see, too, how it can be that,

p. 310. 311 Brandisii

μίαν διώκουσιν ἀλλὰ τὴν κίνησιν. τί οὖν ἅμα τῇ μι- 25
μήσει φασὶν ἐκεῖνο ὁμοίως ὅσοι τε τὸ ἓν καὶ ὅσοι
τοὺς ἀριθμοὺς λέγουσιν; καὶ γὰρ αὐτοὶ τοὺς ἀριθμούς φασιν τὸ ἕν. εἰ δ' ἡ ἔφεσις ἄλλως τε καὶ τοῦ
ἀρίστου μετὰ ψυχῆς, εἰ μή τις λέγοι καθ' ὁμοιό- 5b
τητα καὶ μεταφοράν, ἔμψυχ' ἂν εἴη τὰ κινούμενα·
ψυχῇ δ' ἅμα δοκεῖ καὶ κίνησις ὑπάρχειν· ζωὴ γὰρ
τοῖς ἔχουσιν, ἀφ' ἧς καὶ αἱ ὀρέξεις πρὸς ἕκαστον, ὥσπερ καὶ τοῖς ζῴοις, ἐπεὶ καὶ αἱ αἰσθήσεις 5
καίπερ ἐν τῷ πάσχειν οὖσαι δι' ἑτέρων ὅμως ἐν
9 ψυχῇ γίνονται. εἰ δ' οὖν τῆς κυκλικῆς αἴτιον τὸ
πρῶτον, οὐ τῆς ἀρίστης ἂν εἴη· κρεῖττον γὰρ ἡ
τῆς ψυχῆς, καὶ πρώτη δὴ καὶ μάλιστα ἡ τῆς διανοίας, ἀφ' ἧς καὶ ἡ ὄρεξις. Τάχα δὲ καὶ τοῦτ' ἄν 10
τις ἐπιζητήσειεν, διὰ τί τὰ κυκλικὰ μόνον ἐφετικά,
τῶν δὲ περὶ τὸ μέσον οὐθὲν καίπερ κινητῶν ὄντων, πότερον ὡς ἀδύνατα ἢ ὡς οὐ διικνουμένου
τοῦ πρώτου· ἀλλὰ τοῦτό γ' ἄτοπον, εἰ δι' ἀσθέ-
νειαν· ἰσχυρότερον γὰρ ἄν τις ἀξιώσειεν τοῦ Ὁμή- 15
ρου Διός, ὅς φησιν

αὐτῇ κεν γαίῃ ἐρύσαιμ' αὐτῇ τε θαλάσσῃ.
ἀλλὰ λοιπὸν ὥσπερ ἄδεκτόν τι καὶ ἀσύνετον εἶναι.

5ᵃ 25 μιμήσει] κινήσει ci. Brandis   26 ἐκεῖνο] ἐκεῖνοι corr. B
ὁμοίως om. P   27 αὐτός H   28 εἰ δ' ἡ P: εἰ δὴ J₁C: ἐδὴ RD:
ἔδη BH: ἤδη u
5ᵇ 1 ἀορίστου J₁ (ut vid.) u   λέγει RD   2 μεταφορὰν J rec.
A rec.: διαφορὰν cet.   ἔμψυχ' B₁   3 ψυχῇ corr. Usener: ψυχῆ
P: ψυχὴν C: ψυχή cet.   κίνησιν C   γὰρ] μὲν u   4 αἱ
ὀρέξεις] ὄρεξις O₁u: ὀρέξεις Σ   5 τοῖς ζῴοις ἐπεὶ καὶ αἱ αἰσθήσεις καί-
om. u   τοῖς] τοῦ P₁   αἱ om. Σ   6 ἑτέροις Σ   ὅμως ἐν ψυχῇ
corr. Ross: ὅμως ἔμψυχοι P: ὅμως ἐμψυχοι B₁: ὅμως ἔμψυχοι cet.:
ὅμως ἐμψύχοις Usener: ὅμως ὡς ἐμψύχοις ci. Usener   8 κρεῖττων C:
κρεῖττων Σ   9 ψυχῆς] ψῆς P   δὴ] δέ u   11 ἐπιζητήσει u   12 κοινῇ

though the heavenly bodies have a natural desire, they pursue not rest but motion. Why then is this assertion combined with the stress laid on *imitation*, alike both by those who emphasize the One and by those who emphasize the numbers? For the latter themselves speak of the numbers as imitating the One. And if impulse, especially that towards what is best, involves soul, then unless one is speaking by way of similitude and metaphor, the things that move must be possessed of soul; but with soul movement also seems to be involved; for soul is life to the things that have it, and from this also come the desires towards each object, as in the case of the animals. For even sense-perceptions, though they depend on our being affected by things other than ourselves, yet take place in *soul*. However this may be, if the prime mover is the cause of the circular motion, it will not be the cause of the best motion; for the movement of the soul is better, and first and above all that of thought, from which also springs desire.

And perhaps one might ask this question also, why the rotating bodies alone have impulse, and none of those about the centre of the universe have it, though they are subject to movement: is it because they are incapable of impulse or because the power of the prime mover does not penetrate to them? But this, at any rate, would be strange, if it implied weakness; for one would expect the prime mover to be stronger than Homer's Zeus, who says

I could pull you up, earth, sea, and all.

But the only alternative is that the centre of the

τῶν RD   13 οὐ om. L₁CV²O   17 αὐτῇ κ' ἐν Σ: αὐτίκ' ἐν S
ἐρύσαι μ' u   18 ἀσύνετον corr. Usener: ἀσύνθετον codd.:
ἀσύνδετον ci. Usener

ΘΕΟΦΡΑΣΤΟΥ

p. 311. 312 Brandisii

10 τάχα δὲ πρότερον ζητήσειεν ἄν τις πῶς ἔχει, πότερα μέρη ταῦτα ἢ οὐ μέρη τοῦ οὐρανοῦ, καὶ εἰ μέρη, πῶς μέρη· νῦν γὰρ οἷον ἀπεωσμένα τῶν ἐντιμοτάτων οὐ μόνον κατὰ τὰς χώρας ἀλλὰ καὶ κατὰ τὴν ἐνέργειαν, εἴ περ ἡ κυκλικὴ τοιαύτη· λαμβάνει γὰρ οἷον κατὰ συμβεβηκὸς ὑπὸ τῆς κυκλικῆς περιφορᾶς καὶ εἰς τοὺς τόπους καὶ εἰς ἄλληλα τὰς μεταβολάς. Εἰ δὲ καὶ τὸ ἄριστον ἀπὸ τοῦ ἀρίστου, κάλλιον ἄν τι παρὰ τοῦ πρώτου δέοι τῆς κυκλοφορίας, εἰ μὴ ἄρ' ἐκωλύετο τῷ μὴ δύνασθαι δέχεσθαι· τὸ γὰρ δὴ πρῶτον καὶ θειότατον πάντα τὰ ἄριστα βουλόμενον. τάχα δὲ τοῦτο μὲν οἷον ὑπερβατόν τι καὶ ἀζήτητον· ἀξιοῖ γὰρ ὁ τοῦτο λέγων ἅπανθ' ὅμοια καὶ ἐν τοῖς ἀρίστοις εἶναι, 11 μικράν τιν' | ἢ μηδεμίαν ἔχοντα διαφοράν. Τόδε δ' ἄν τις ἴσως ἀπορήσειεν πρὸς αὐτὸν τὸν πρῶτον οὐρανὸν ἀναφέρων, πότερον ἡ περιφορὰ τῆς οὐσίας ἐστὶν αὐτοῦ καὶ ἅμα τῷ πεπαῦσθαι φθείροιτ' ἄν, ἢ εἴ περ ἐφέσει τινὶ καὶ ὀρέξει, κατὰ συμβεβηκός· εἰ μὴ ἄρα σύμφυτον αὐτῷ τὸ ὀρέγεσθαι— καὶ οὐθὲν κωλύει τοιαῦτ' ἄττα τῶν ὄντων ὑπάρχειν. ἴσως δ' ἂν εἴη καὶ ἀφελόντα τὴν ὄρεξιν ὑπὲρ αὐτῆς τῆς κινήσεως ἀπορεῖν, εἰ ἀφαιρεθεῖσα

5^b 20 οὐρανοῦ] ἀνθρώπου Σ   22 ἐντιμωτάτων J   καὶ om. J₁
23 λαμβάνει corr. Usener : συμβαίνει codd.   24 οἷον] εἶναι ci.
Zeller   25 περιφορᾷ RB₁D : περιφορ^{αν} H   26 μεταβολάς]
μεταβολὰς ἔχειν ci. Camotius   τὸ ἄριστον ἀπὸ τοῦ spatio relicto
omittunt RBH₁D   27 περὶ C   28 κυκλοφωρίας R   τῷ
om. u

6^a 1 δὴ] δεῖ J   2 βουλόμεν^{ως} H : βουλόμενον ἦν J rec.   3 τι]
τε Σ   4 εἶναι μικράν τιν'] εἶναι τὰ χείριστα μικράν τιν' J rec. : μικρὰν
εἶναι τινὰ Σ   6 ἀπορήσειεν ἴσως LC   8 φθείροι τ' u

universe should be, as it were, something irreceptive and unintelligent. Perhaps, however, one might first inquire what manner of being the things at the centre have, whether they are or are not parts of the celestial system, and if they are parts, how they are so; for in this account they are as it were thrust apart from the things of highest worth not only in spatial position but also in their activity, *if* the rotatory movement is the highest activity; for they acquire as it were by accident under the influence of the rotation their changes both into their own places and into one another.

And if from the best comes the best, the heavenly bodies should derive something finer than the rotation from the prime mover, unless indeed they were prevented by not being able to receive anything better; for surely that which is first and most divine is something that wishes for everything that is best. But perhaps this is, as it were, something extravagant and not to be looked for; for he who says this demands that everything should be alike and of the best, having little or no difference.

One might perhaps raise this question, with reference to the first heaven itself, whether its rotation is of its essence and with the cessation of this it would perish, or whether, if the rotation depends on an impulse and desire, it is not merely incidental; unless indeed desire is innate in the first heaven—and there is nothing to prevent some things from being of this nature. And it would perhaps be possible, too, waiving the question of the desire, to inquire about the motion itself, whether if it were removed it would destroy the heavens.

δέγεσθαι J₁   11 αττι P : άτα C   13 εἰ ex corr. J rec. (quid habuit J₁ incertum) : εἰ P : οἱ C₁

p. 312. 313 Brandisii
φθείροι ἂν τὸν οὐρανόν. Καὶ τοῦτο μὲν ὥσπερ ἑτέρων λόγων. ἀπὸ δ' οὖν ταύτης ἢ τούτων τῶν

III ἀρχῶν ἀξιώσειεν ἄν τις (τάχα δὲ καὶ ἀπὸ τῶν ἄλλων ἄρ', ἄν τις τίθηται) τὰ ἐφεξῆς εὐθὺς ἀποδιδόναι καὶ μὴ μέχρι του προελθόντα παύεσθαι· τοῦτο γὰρ τελέου καὶ φρονοῦντος, ὅ περ Ἀρχύτας ποτ' ἔφη ποιεῖν Εὔρυτον διατιθέντα τινὰς ψήφους· λέγειν γὰρ ὡς ὅδε μὲν ἀνθρώπου ὁ ἀριθμός, ὅδε δὲ ἵππου, ὅδε δ' ἄλλου τινὸς τυγχάνει. νῦν δ' οἵ γε πολλοὶ μέχρι τινὸς ἐλθόντες καταπαύονται, καθάπερ καὶ οἱ τὸ ἓν καὶ τὴν ἀόριστον δυάδα ποιοῦντες· τοὺς γὰρ ἀριθμοὺς γεννήσαντες καὶ τὰ ἐπίπεδα καὶ τὰ σώματα σχεδὸν τἆλλα παραλείπουσιν πλὴν ὅσον ἐφαπτόμενοι καὶ τοσοῦτο μόνον δηλοῦντες, ὅτι τὰ μὲν ἀπὸ τῆς ἀορίστου δυάδος, οἷον τόπος καὶ κενὸν καὶ ἄπειρον, τὰ δ' ἀπὸ τῶν ἀριθμῶν καὶ τοῦ ἑνός, οἷον ψυχὴ καὶ ἄλλ' ἄττα· χρόνον δ' ἅμα καὶ οὐρανὸν καὶ ἕτερα δὴ πλείω, τοῦ δ' οὐρανοῦ πέρι καὶ τῶν λοιπῶν οὐδεμίαν ἔτι ποιοῦνται μνείαν· ὡσαύτως δ' οἱ περὶ Σπεύσιππον, οὐδὲ τῶν ἄλλων οὐθεὶς πλὴν Ξενοκράτης· οὗτος γὰρ ἅπαντά πως περιτίθησιν περὶ τὸν κόσμον, ὁμοίως αἰσθητὰ καὶ νοητὰ καὶ μαθηματικὰ καὶ ἔτι δὴ τὰ θεῖα. πειρᾶται δὲ καὶ

6ᵃ 14 φθείροιτ' RD : φθείροιτο BH   15 ἀπὸ PJ : αὐτὺ Σ   17 ἀρ' ἄν τις P : αρ (ut vid.) ἄν τις J₁ : ἆς (ut vid.) ἄν τις J rec. (an recte?) : ὃς (in spatio vacuo addidit manus antiqua) ἄν τις L : 'ἄρ' ἄν τις C : ἄν τις ἄρα ci. Usener : ἀρχῶν, ἄν τις Wimmer   τιθῆται τὰς Σ   18 τοῦ προελθόντας L : τοῦ προελθόντος CΣ   παύσασθαι R   19 ὅπερ P : ὅπως Σ   21 λέγει LC   γὰρ om. J   22 δὲ ἵππου, ὅδε om. Σ   ἀλλ' οὗ τινος R   26 καὶ alt. om. J corr. L : ποιοῦντες R₁   τἆλλα corr.

ΤΩΝ ΜΕΤΑ ΤΑ ΦΥΣΙΚΑ ΙΙ

This indeed belongs, as it were, to a different set of problems. But at any rate, starting from this first principle or these first principles, one might demand (and presumably also from any other first principles that may be assumed) that they should go straight on to give an account of the successive derivatives, and not proceed to a certain point and then stop; for this is the part of a competent and sensible man, to do what Archytas once said Eurytus did as he arranged certain pebbles; he said (according to Archytas) that this is in fact the number of man, and this of horse, and this of something else. But now *most* people go to a certain point and then stop, as those do also who set up the One and the indefinite dyad; for after generating numbers and planes and solids they leave out almost everything else, except to the extent of just touching on them and making this much, and only this much, plain, that some things proceed from the indefinite dyad, e.g. place, the void, and the infinite, and others from the numbers and the One, e. g. soul and certain other things; and they generate simultaneously time and the heavens and several other things, but of the heavens and the remaining things in the universe they make no further mention; and similarly the school of Speusippus does not do so, nor does any of the other philosophers except Xenocrates; for *he* does somehow assign everything its place in the universe, alike objects of sense, objects of reason or mathematical objects, and divine

Brandis: τὰ ἄλλα P: τ' ἄλλα JCB: τἄλλα RHD   27 ὅσων J
6ᵇ 3-4 χρόνον ... πλείω om. J corr. L: secluserunt Ritter, Usener
3 δ'] θ' ci. Usener   5 οὐδὲ μίαν J corr. C: οὐδὲ μένων RB₁HD
ποιοῦν^τ (i.e. ποιοῦντα) Σ u   6 οἱ] οὐδ' οἱ J: οὐδεῒ L: οὐδὐοί C
πεύσιππον C: σπεύσιππον RB,D   7 οὗτος P: οὕτως CR   γὰρ]
γὰρ ἂν J₁   διατιθῇσιν ci. Usener (an recte?)   9 δή] δὲ u

ΘΕΟΦΡΑΣΤΟΥ

p. 313 Brandisii

Ἑστιαῖος μέχρι τινός, οὐχ ὥσπερ εἴρηται περὶ τῶν πρώτων μόνον. Πλάτων μὲν οὖν ἐν τῷ ἀνάγειν εἰς τὰς ἀρχὰς δόξειεν ἂν ἅπτεσθαι τῶν ἄλλων εἰς τὰς ἰδέας ἀνάπτων, ταύτας δ' εἰς τοὺς ἀριθμούς, ἐκ δὲ τούτων εἰς τὰς ἀρχάς, εἶτα κατὰ τὴν γένεσιν μέχρι τῶν εἰρημένων· οἱ δὲ τῶν ἀρχῶν μόνον. ἔνιοι δὲ καὶ τὴν ἀλήθειαν ἐν τούτοις· τὰ γὰρ ὄντα μόνον περὶ τὰς ἀρχάς. συμβαίνει δὲ τοὐναντίον ἢ ἐν ταῖς ἄλλαις μεθόδοις· ἐν ἐκείνοις γὰρ τὰ μετὰ τὰς ἀρχὰς ἰσχυρότερα καὶ οἷον τελεώτερα τῶν ἐπιστημῶν· τάχα δὲ καὶ εὐλόγως· ἔνθα μὲν γὰρ τῶν ἀρχῶν, ἐν δὲ ταῖς λοιπαῖς ἀπὸ τῶν ἀρχῶν ἡ ζήτησις.

IV 14 Πῶς δέ ποτε χρὴ καὶ ποίας τὰς ἀρχὰς ὑποθέσθαι, τάχ' ἂν ἀπορήσειέν τις, πότερον ἀμόρφους καὶ οἷον δυναμικάς, ὥσπερ ὅσοι πῦρ καὶ γῆν, ἢ μεμορφωμένας, ὡς μάλιστα δέον ταύτας ὡρίσθαι, καθάπερ ἐν τῷ Τιμαίῳ φησίν· τοῖς γὰρ τιμιωτάτοις οἰκειότατον ἡ τάξις καὶ τὸ ὡρίσθαι. φαίνεται δὲ καὶ ἐν ταῖς λοιπαῖς σχεδὸν ἔχειν οὕτω, καθάπερ ἐν γραμματικῇ καὶ μουσικῇ καὶ ταῖς μαθηματικαῖς, συνακολουθεῖ δὲ καὶ τὰ μετὰ τὰς ἀρχάς· ἔτι δὲ καὶ κατὰ τὰς τέχνας ὁμοίως,

6ᵇ 10 ἐστι αἶος P : ἑστιαῖος RD   τινσος P   11 μόνων Σ
12 ἀρχὰς] ἀρχὰς τὰ ὑπὸ τὰς ἀρχὰς J rec. L   δόξειεν ἄν] δόξει ἐρᾶν J
14 ἀργάς P   εἰ τα P   κατά] κατάγων Usener   16 μόνων Σ
19 ἐκείναις Camotius   20 post ἐπιστημῶν J rec. in marg. add.
ἐνταῦθα δὲ τὸ κράτιστον ἡ ἀρχή   21 ἔνθα] ἐνταῦθα J rec.   23
καὶ ποίας] ὁποίας RB₁HD (καὶ supra add. B)   24 ἀπορρήσειέ BHD
ὁμόρφους H   27-8 καθάπερ...ὡρίσθαι om. C   28 οἰκειώτατον JΣ
7ᵃ 2 ἐν γραμματικῇ καὶ μουσικῇ J rec. : ἡ γραμματικὴ καὶ μουσικὴ

things as well. And Hestiaeus too tries, up to a point, 13 and does not speak, in the way we have described, only about the first principles. Now Plato in reducing things to the ruling principles might seem to be treating of the other things in linking them up with the Ideas, and these with the numbers, and in proceeding from the numbers to the ruling principles, and then, following the order of generation, down as far as the things we have named; but the others treat of the ruling principles only. And some even find the truth of things only in these; for they concentrate reality entirely in the ruling principles. But this is the very opposite of what happens in all other studies; for in them the parts of the science that come after the ruling principles are more powerful and, as it were, more complete; and perhaps this is even what might reasonably be expected; for here the search is for the ruling principles, but in other studies it proceeds from the ruling principles.

One might perhaps raise the question how, after IV 14 all, we should conceive of the ruling principles and of what nature we should suppose them to be,— whether shapeless and as it were merely potential (as those conceive of them who make fire and earth the ruling principles), or already possessed of shape, on the ground that these, if anything, should be definite, as Plato says in the *Timaeus*; for order and definiteness are most appropriate to the things of highest worth. And in the other sciences this seems pretty much to be so, as for instance in grammar and music and the mathematical sciences; and the things that come after the first principles follow suit; and

PJ₁Σ: ἡ μουσικὴ καὶ ἡ γραμματικὴ ⌐C   3 συνακολουσθεῖ P: συνακολουθεῖν Usener   4 τὰς alt. om. Σ u

p. 313. 314 Brandisii

αἵ περ τὴν φύσιν μιμοῦνται, καὶ τὰ ὄργανα | καὶ
τὰ ἄλλα κατὰ τὰς ἀρχάς. οἱ μὲν οὖν ἐμμόρφους
πάσας, οἱ δὲ μόνον τὰς ὑλικάς· οἱ δ' ἄμφω, τάς
τ' ἐμμόρφους καὶ τὰς τῆς ὕλης, ὡς ἐν ἀμφοῖν
τὸ τέλεον ⟨ὄν⟩· οἷον γὰρ ἐξ ἀντικειμένων τὴν
ἅπασαν οὐσίαν. ἄλογον δὲ κἀκείνοις δόξειεν ἄν,
εἰ ὁ μὲν ὅλος οὐρανὸς καὶ ἕκαστα τῶν μερῶν
ἅπαντ' ἐν τάξει καὶ λόγῳ καὶ μορφαῖς καὶ δυνάμεσιν καὶ περιόδοις, ἐν δὲ ταῖς ἀρχαῖς μηθὲν
τοιοῦτον ἀλλ' "ὥσπερ σάρμα εἰκῇ κεχυμένων ὁ
κάλλιστος", φησὶν Ἡράκλειτος, "[ὁ] κόσμος". καὶ
κατὰ τοὐλάχιστον δ' ὡς εἰπεῖν λαμβάνουσιν ὁμοίως
ἐν ἀψύχοις καὶ ἐμψύχοις· ὡρισμέναι γὰρ ἑκάστων
αἱ φύσεις ὡς εἰπεῖν καί περ αὐτομάτως γινομέ-
νων· τὰς δ' ἀρχὰς ἀορίστους εἶναι. Χαλεπὸν δὲ
πάλιν αὖ τὸ τοὺς λόγους ἑκάστοις περιθεῖναι
πρὸς τὸ ἕνεκά του συνάγοντας ἐν ἅπασιν, καὶ ἐν
ζῴοις καὶ φυτοῖς καὶ ἐν αὐτῇ πομφόλυγι· πλὴν
εἰ συμβαίνει τῇ ἑτέρων τάξει καὶ μεταβολῇ μορ-
φάς τε παντοίας καὶ ποικιλίας γίνεσθαι τῶν περὶ
τὸν ἀέρα καὶ τὴν γῆν· ὧν δὴ μέγιστόν τινες παρά-

7ᵃ 6 ἐνμόρφους P : ἀμόρφους O : εὐμόρφους Σ   7 πάσας] πάσας τίθενται J rec. L   μόνον] μόνον ἀμόρφους J rec. L   8 τε ἀμόρφους Σ   9 τέλειον Σ   ὄν inseruit Usener   10 κἀκεῖνο ci. Bergk   12 ἅπαντ'] ἅπαντά τ' Σ   14 σάρμα corr. Diels : σάρξ codd. : σάρον ci. Bernays : σωρὸς ci. Usener   κεχυμένον Usener   15 ὁ del. Usener   15–19 καὶ . . . εἶναι seclusit Usener 'non ut spuria sed ut relicta ex altera proximae sententiae (v. 10–15) eaque ampliore forma'   16 τοὐλάχιστου P : τοῦ λάχιστον C : τοῦ ἐλάχιστον Σ : τὰ τοῦ ἐλάχιστον u   17 καὶ ἐμψύχοις om. u   19 τὰς δ'] τὰς J₁ : οἱ τὰς J rec. : εἰς τὰς L   χαλεπὸν] λέγουσι. λεκτέον L : λεπὸν C   20 αὖ τὸ corr. Zeller : αὐτὸ codd. : αὐτὸ τὸ ci. Brandis   ἑκάστους u

again similarly in the case of the arts, which imitate nature, both the instruments and everything else depend on the ruling principles. Some thinkers, then, make all the ruling principles to be possessed of form, while others recognize only the material principles; and others recognize both, both the formal principles and those of matter, on the ground that complete reality involves both; for they make substance as a whole to be composed, as it were, of opposites. But even those who make the ruling principles material would think it unreasonable if the whole universe and each of its parts all involve order and plan in respect both of shapes and of powers and of periods of time, but in the ruling principles there is nothing of this sort, but 'the most fair universe', as Heraclitus says, 'is like a rubbish-heap of things thrown anyhow.' Yet they make the assumption we have named, even (one may say) in the smallest detail, alike among inanimate and animate things; for the natures of each set of things, so to speak, are definite—even when the things come into being spontaneously—but the ruling principles, they say, are indefinite.

On the other hand, it is difficult to assign plans to each class of things, linking them up with their final cause in all cases, both in animals and in plants and in the very bubble; unless it happens by reason of the order and change of *other* things that all manner of shapes and varieties arise of things in the air and on the earth ; of which some make the greatest example to be the facts about the seasons of the year,

---

21 συναγόνας RB₁HD   22 παμφόλυγι J : παμφόλυγγι C   23
ἑτέρων] ἀστέρων Usener   μεταβωλῆι (ut vid.) P₁: μεταβολὴ C
7ᵇ 1 τε] τὰς Σ : om. u   ποικίλας J corr. LC   2 δή] τι u

18 ΘΕΟΦΡΑΣΤΟΥ

p. 314. 315 Brandisii

δεῖγμα ποιοῦνται τὰ περὶ τὰς ὥρας τὰς ἐτησίους, ἐν αἷς καὶ ζῴων καὶ φυτῶν καὶ καρπῶν γενέσεις, οἷον γεννῶντος τοῦ ἡλίου. καὶ ταῦτα μὲν ἐνταῦθά που ζητεῖ τὴν σκέψιν, ἀφορισμὸν ἀπαιτοῦντα μέχρι πόσου τὸ τεταγμένον, καὶ διὰ τί τὸ πλέον ἀδύνατον ἢ εἰς τὸ χεῖρον ἡ μετάβασις.

V 16 | Ἐν δὲ ταῖς ἀρχαῖς, ὅθεν δὴ καὶ ὁ πρῶτος λόγος, εἰκότως ἄν τις καὶ τὸ περὶ τῆς ἠρεμίας ἀπορήσειεν. εἰ μὲν γὰρ ὡς βέλτιον, ἀνάψειεν ἂν ταῖς ἀρχαῖς· εἰ δ' ὡς ἀργία καὶ στέρησίς τις κινήσεως, οὐκ ἀνάψει, ἀλλ' εἴ περ, τὴν ἐνέργειαν ἀντιμεταλλακτέον ὡς προτέραν καὶ τιμιωτέραν, τὴν δὲ κίνησιν ἐν τοῖς αἰσθητοῖς· ἐπεὶ τό γε διὰ τοῦτ' ἠρεμεῖν ὡς ἀδύνατον ἀεὶ κινούμενον εἶναι τὸ κινοῦν — οὐ γὰρ ἂν εἴη πρῶτον — κίνδυνος μὴ λογῶδες, καὶ ἄλλως οὐκ ἀξιόπιστον, ἀλλὰ μείζω τινὰ αἰτίαν ζητεῖ. δοκεῖ δὲ καὶ ἡ αἴσθησις τρόπον τινὰ συναυδᾶν ὡς ἐνδεχόμενον μὴ ἀεὶ τὸ κινοῦν ἕτερον εἶναι καὶ ὃ κινεῖ διὰ τὸ ποιεῖν καὶ πάσχειν· ἔτι δ' ἐάν τις ἐπ' αὐτὸν ἄγῃ τὸν

7ᵇ 3 ποιοῦνται P: ποιοῦντες RB₁HD   ἐτησίους corr. Usener: ἐστησίους P: αἰτίους JC: ἐτείους Σ   5 οἷον P: οἷον ἡ C   6 ποῦ ζητεῖ J: ζητεῖ L: ζητεῖν C: ζητεῖ ποῦ Σ   ἀφορισμὸν RBD: ἀφωσισμὸν H: ἀφοσιασμὸν u   8 τὸ om. Σ   ἢ J rec. B marg. (quid habuerit J₁ incertum): εἰ P: ἡ RB₁HD: εἰ CA   ἡ om. Σ   9 ἀρχᾶς (ut vid.) P₁   10 ἠρεμίας PJ corr. C: ἠρομίας (ut vid.) J₁   11 ἀνάψειεν ἂν] ἀνάψει ἐν J₁ (ut vid.) u: ἀνάψιεν ἂν R   12 ἀρχᾶς P: ἀρχαῖς· ὅθεν δὴ καὶ ὁ πρῶτος λόγος εἰκότως ἄν τις καὶ τὸ περὶ τῆς ἠρεμίας ἀπορήσει C   τις P: τῆς cet.   13 ἀντιμεταλλακτέον] τι μεταλλακτέον PJC corr.: τὴν μεταλλακτέον C₁: ἀντικαταλλακτέον Usener   14 προτέραν] ex περτέραν (ut vid.) corr. P₁   15 ἐν seclusit Usener   τοῦτ' ἠρεμεῖν J₁: τοῦθ' ἠρεμεῖν δεῖ corr. J: τοῦθ' ἠρεμεῖν C   16 κινούμενον corr. Ross: κινοῦν codd.   εἶναι τὸ κινοῦν in spatio 7 litterarum J₁ (ἄτοπον marg. J rec.): εἶναι τὸ κινού-

on which depends the generation both of animals and of plants and fruits, the sun being, as it were, the begetter. And these subjects call for inquiry somewhere hereabout, demanding a definition of the extent to which order prevails, and an account of the reason why more of it is impossible or the change it would produce would be for the worse.

In regard to the ruling principles, which were the starting-point of our first remarks, one might naturally raise the problem of the immobility ascribed to them. If it is treated as a better state, one would attach it to the ruling principles; but if it is treated as inertness and privation of motion, one will not attach it to them, but if one ascribes anything but motion to them, 'activity' instead must be substituted for 'motion' as something prior and of higher worth, and motion must be said to be present only in objects of sense; since to say that things are at rest for *this* reason, that it is impossible that the mover at each stage should be itself in motion—for then it would not be primary—may be suspected to be a merely verbal argument, and on other grounds not worthy of belief; the view demands a greater justification than this. And even sense-perception seems in a way to join in proclaiming that the mover need not always, because the one acts and the other is acted on, be different from what it moves; the same result follows if we apply the question to reason itself and to God. Strange too is the other thing that has been maintained—that the things that desire what is at rest do

μενον Usener   17 οὐ γὰρ in spatio vel rasura unius litt. J₁   πρῶτον καὶ κίνδυνος J rec. L : κίνδυνος πρῶτον Σ   18 λογω⁴ιδες J : λογοειδὲς CΣ   19 καὶ om. P   τρόπον] πρότερον BH u   20 μὴ ἀεὶ corr. Wimmer : μὴ δεῖ PJ : καὶ ὡς δεῖ L : μὴ δὴ CΣ   21 κινεῖται interpres, Usener   ποιοῦν Usener : an τὸ ποιοῦν ?   22 ἔτι δὲ ἂν JCΣ : ἔστι δὲ ἂν u   ἄγει JC : ἀνάγῃ ci. Usener

ΘΕΟΦΡΑΣΤΟΥ

p. 315. 316 Brandisii

νοῦν καὶ τὸν θεόν. ἄτοπον δὲ καὶ τὸ ἕτερον λεχθέν, ὡς οὐ μιμοῦνται τὰ ὀρεγόμενα τοῦ ἠρεμοῦντος· τί γὰρ αὐτοῖς οὐ συνακολουθεῖ ἡ τῶν ἄλλων; πλὴν ἴσως οὐχ ὁμοίως ληπτέον ὡς εἰς τὸ ἀμερὲς ἄγοντας, ἀλλ' ὅπως ὅ τι μάλιστα σύμφωνον ἑαυτῷ καὶ ἀπηρτισμένον ὡς ἂν πόλις ἢ ζῷον ἢ ἄλλο τι τῶν μεριστῶν ᾖ καὶ ὁ ὅλος οὐρανός, ὃν δή φασιν εἶναι τελεώτατον.

VI 17 Ἐπιποθεῖ δέ τινα καὶ τὰ τοιάδε λόγον, πῶς ποτε τῶν ὄντων ὁ μερισμὸς εἰς ὕλην καὶ μορφήν, πότερον ὡς τὸ μὲν ὄν, τὸ δὲ μὴ ὄν, δυνάμει δ' ὂν καὶ | ἀγόμενον εἰς ἐνέργειαν· ἢ ὂν μέν, ἀόριστον δὲ καθά περ ἐν ταῖς τέχναις, ᾗ δὲ γένεσις, ἡ οὐσία γ' αὐτῶν τῷ μορφοῦσθαι κατὰ τοὺς λόγους· ἀλλ' οὕτω γ' εἰς μὲν τὸ βέλτιον τάχ' ἂν ἡ μετάβασις εἴη, τὸ δ' εἶναι οὐθὲν ἂν ἧττον ἀληθὲς ὑπάρχοι κατ' αὐτήν (οὐ γὰρ ἂν οὐδὲ γίνοιτο μὴ ὑπαρχούσης), ἀλλὰ τὸ μήτε τόδε μήτε ποιὸν μήτε ποσόν, ὡς ἀόριστον τοῖς εἴδεσιν, δύναμιν δέ τιν' ἔχον. ὅλως δὲ κατ' ἀναλογίαν ληπτέον ἐπὶ τὰς τέχνας καὶ εἴ τις ὁμοιότης ἄλλη.

8[a] 1 κινοῦνται interpres, Usener   τοῦ ἠρεμοῦντος] τὰ ἠρεμοῦντα supra add. J rec.   2 τί corr. Usener : εἰ J$_1$ cet. : ἢ J corr. L   αὐτοῖς] ἂν τοῖς Usener   οὐ συνακολουθεῖ ἡ corr. Ross : οὐσιν ἀκολουθεῖ ἡ P : οὐσιν ἀκολουθείη cet. : οὐσιν ἀκολουθοίη ci. Sylburg   5 ἢ (post ζῷον) P : ἡ J : ἡ καὶ Σ   6 ᾖ corr. Usener : ἢ PJ : ἡ cet.   καὶ] καὶ καὶ J   ὁ ὅλος] ὅλος Σ : ὅλως u   7 τελεώτατον u   11 δ' ὂν B rec. : δ' ἐν P : δ' ἐν JCRB$_1$HD : δὲ ὂν O   12 δέ] δίον RHD : δὲ ὂν B u   12–14 τέχναις, ᾗ . . . ἀλλ' corr. Ross : τέχναις ἡ . . . ἀλλ' codd. (pro τῷ l. 13 τῶν J corr. C : τὸ Σ) : τέχναις. εἰ . . . ἀλλ' Usener : τέχναις. εἰ δὲ γένεσις ἡ οὐσία γε αὐτῶν τὸ μορφοῦσθαι κατὰ τοὺς λόγους, ἀλλ' ci. Usener : an τέχναις ᾗ γένεσις, ἡ οὐσία δ' (vel τέχναις, ᾗ δὲ γένεσις ἡ οὐσία γ') αὐτῶν τῷ μορφοῦσθαι κατὰ τοὺς λόγους· ἀλλ' ?   15 οὐθὲν P : αθὲν (spatio antecedente) V^{a}O : ἀθὲν R$_1$B$_1$HD

not imitate its immobility; for why does not, for those thinkers, the immobility of all other things follow on that of the first mover? Only, perhaps, we should not understand the matter as if we were reducing the universe to something that has no parts; we should only aim at securing that the whole universe, which they do maintain to be most perfect, shall be as far as possible harmonious with itself, and well fitted together as though it were a city or an animal or something else that *has* parts.

The following problems also want some discussion—how the division of things into matter and form is to be understood; are we to take the one as being and the other as not-being, but as being potentially and being drawn towards actuality; or to say that it is being, but indeterminate, as is the material used in the arts, and that where there is generation, the *essence* of the things generated depends on their being shaped in accordance with their definitions? But on *this* showing, while the change would perhaps be a change for the better, yet, none the less, being would already be truly predicable of things in virtue of their matter (for the things would not even come into being if it did not pre-exist), but there would be only that which is neither a particular thing nor of a particular quality or quantity, as being indeterminate in its specific characteristics, but having a certain potentiality. And in general we must understand matter by virtue of an analogy with the arts, or any other similarity that may exist.

16 ὑπάρχει (ὑπαρχ' D) CRD : ὑπάρχων B : ὑπάρχων H : ὑπάρχειν u καταυτήν P : καθ' αὑτήν JC corr. B₁HD : καθ' αὑτήν C₁   18 ποιόν] τὸ ποιόν LC   20 ληπτέον] ἀνιτέον ci. Usener   ἐπὶ P : ἐστὶ Usener   εἰ] ἢ P

22 ΘΕΟΦΡΑΣΤΟΥ

p. 316. 317 Brandisii

VII 18 Δόξειεν δ' ἂν καὶ τοῦτ' ἔχειν ἀπορίαν, εἰ μὴ ἄρα περιεργίαν τοῦ ζητεῖν, τί δή ποτε ἡ φύσις καὶ ἡ ὅλη δ' οὐσία τοῦ παντὸς ἐν ἐναντίοις ἐστίν, καὶ σχεδὸν ἰσομοιρεῖ τὸ χεῖρον τῷ βελτίονι, μᾶλλον δὲ καὶ πολλῷ πλέον ἐστίν, ὥστε δοκεῖν καὶ Εὐριπίδην καθόλου λέγειν ὡς "οὐκ ἂν γένοιτο χωρὶς ἐσθλά". ὁ δὲ τοιοῦτος λόγος ἐγγὺς τοῦ ζητεῖν ὅ τι οὐ πάντ' ἀγαθὰ οὐδὲ πάντα ὅμοια, καὶ ὅ τι κατὰ πάντων μὲν τὸ εἶναι λέγομεν, οὐθὲν δὲ ὅμοιον ἀλλήλοις, καθά περ τὰ λευκὰ καὶ μέλανα, ἐν αὑτοῖς. ἔτι δὲ τὸ δοκοῦν παραδοξότερον, ὡς οὐχ οἷόν τε τὸ ὂν ἄνευ τῶν ἐναντίων. οἱ δ' ἔτι πλέονι τῷ παραδόξῳ χρώμενοι καὶ τὸ μὴ ὂν μηδὲ γεγονὸς μηδὲ μέλλον προσκαταριθμοῦσιν εἰς τὴν τοῦ παντὸς φύσιν. ἀλλ' ἥδε μὲν οἷον ὑπερβατός τις σοφία.

VIII 19 Τὸ δὲ ὂν ὅτι πολλαχῶς, φανερόν· ἡ γὰρ αἴσθησις καὶ τὰς διαφορὰς θεωρεῖ καὶ τὰς αἰτίας ζητεῖ· | τάχα δ' ἀληθέστερον εἰπεῖν ὡς ὑποβάλλει τῇ διανοίᾳ τὰ μὲν ἁπλῶς ζητοῦσα, τὰ δ' ἀπορίαν ἐνεργαζομένη, δι' ἧς, κἂν μὴ δύνηται προβαίνειν, ὅμως ἐμφαίνεταί τι φῶς ἐν τῷ μὴ φωτὶ ζητούντων ἐπὶ πλέον. τὸ ἐπίστασθαι ἄρα οὐκ ἄνευ διαφορᾶς τινος. εἴ τε γὰρ ἕτερα ἀλλήλων, διαφορά τις· ἔν τε τοῖς καθόλου πλειόνων ὄντων τῶν ὑπὸ

8ᵃ 22 περιέργειαν JC   τοῦ ζητεῖν iterat P   23 ἐν om. CΣ
25 πολὺ BH u   26 οὐκ ex οὐδ' corr. P₁
8ᵇ 4 τὰ μέλανα Σ   ἔτι δέ] ἔτι δὲ καὶ Σ : ἔστι καὶ u₁ : ἔτι καὶ corr.
u : ἔστι δὲ καὶ ed. Aldina pr.   6 δέτι J   πλέον u   7 ὂν ex ὢν (ut vid.) corr. P   γεγονὼς J₁ : γεγονὸς C₁   9 ὑπερβατή u
12 ὑπερβάλλει (ὑπερβαλλ') CBH) JCBHD : ὑπερβάλλων R : ὑπερ-

But this too would seem to involve a difficulty, VII 18 unless indeed it be a superfluity of inquisitiveness to ask the question: Why is it that nature, and indeed the whole substance of the universe, consists of contraries, and the worse has practically an equal share in it with the better, or rather is much greater, so that Euripides, too, would seem to be speaking universally when he says that 'good things cannot come to pass alone'? But such a way of speaking comes near to inquiring why things are not all good or all alike, and why, while we assert being of all things, there is no likeness to one another in them, as there is between white things and black things. And the opinion that being *cannot* exist without contraries is still more paradoxical. Some indulge in paradox yet further and count in to the nature of the universe that which is not and has not been and is not going to be. But this is, one may say, a transcendent sort of wisdom.

That 'being' has more than one sense, however, VIII 19 is evident; for sense-perception both views the differences and seeks their causes; though perhaps it is truer to say that it provides thought with material, partly by simple inquiry, partly by producing in us suspense of mind, through which, even if thought cannot advance, yet some light makes its appearance in our non-light as we search further. Knowledge, then, does not exist without some difference. For if things are other than one another, there is a difference; and within universals, the things that fall under the universals being more than one,

βάλλοντα u   14 ἐνεργαζομένηι J: ἐργαζομένη CRBcorr. D: ἐργαζομένην B₁H   παραβαίνειν Σ   15 τῷ] τὸ J   φωτίζητούτων R
16 ἄρα] ἐστιν LÇ   17 εἰ P: ᾗ Usener

p. 317. 318 Brandisii

τὰ καθόλου διαφέρειν ἀνάγκη καὶ ταῦτα, ἐάν τε γένη τὰ καθόλου ἐάν τ' εἴδη. σχεδὸν δὲ καὶ ἐπιστήμη πᾶσα τῶν ἰδίων· ἥ τε γὰρ οὐσία καὶ τὸ τί ἦν εἶναι καθ' ἕκαστον ἴδιον, τά τε θεωρούμενα καθ' ἑαυτὰ καὶ οὐ κατὰ συμβεβηκὸς ἦν ἂν τὶ κατὰ τινός. ὅλως δὲ τὸ ἐν πλείοσιν τὸ αὐτὸ συνιδεῖν ἐπιστήμης, ἤτοι κοινῇ καὶ καθόλου λεγόμενον ἢ ἰδίᾳ πως καθ' ἕκαστον, οἷον ἀριθμοῖς γραμμαῖς, ζῴοις φυτοῖς· τέλεος δ' ἡ ἐξ ἀμφοῖν. ἔστιν δ' ἐνίων μὲν καθόλου τέλος (ἐν τούτῳ γὰρ τὸ αἴτιον), τῶν δὲ τὸ ἐν μέρει, καθ' ὅσα διαίρεσις εἰς τὰ ἄτομα, καθά περ ἐν τοῖς πρακτοῖς καὶ ποιητοῖς· οὕτως γὰρ αὐτῶν ἡ ἐνέργεια. Ταὐτῷ δ' ἐπιστάμεθα καὶ οὐσίᾳ καὶ ἀριθμῷ καὶ εἴδει καὶ γένει καὶ ἀναλογίᾳ καὶ εἰ ἄρα παρὰ ταῦτα διαιρέσεις· διὰ πλεῖστου δὲ τὸ κατ' ἀναλογίαν, ὡς ἂν ἀπέχοντος πλεῖστον, τὰ μὲν δι' ἡμᾶς αὐτούς, τὰ δὲ διὰ τὸ ὑποκείμενον, τὰ δὲ διὰ τἄμφω.

Πλεοναχῶς δ' ὄντος τοῦ ἐπίστασθαι, πῶς | ἕκαστα μεταδιωκτέον; ἀρχὴ καὶ μέγιστον ὁ οἰκεῖος τρόπος, οἷον τὰ πρῶτα καὶ νοητά, καὶ τὰ κινητὰ

8ᵇ 20 γένει ... εἴδει PJC   24 ὁμοίως Usener: an ὅμως? πλείωσιν P: πείοσι B₁H   25 καὶ om. J   λέγομεν Σ   26 ἀριθμοῦ BH u: ἀριθμῷ interpres   27 τέλεος δ' ἡ P: τέλος δὲ cet.: τέλος δ' ἡ Brandis

9ᵃ 1 ἐνίων μὲν corr. Ross: ἔνια τῶν J₁: ἔνια τῶν μὲν J corr. m. 1 cet.: ἐνίων μὲν τὸ Wimmer: ἔνθα τῶν μὲν Usener   2 δὲ τὸ] δ' ci. Usener   3 πρακτικοῖς LC: om. u   4 ταυτωι P: ταὐτὸ cet.   6 εἰ ἄρα] ἔτι L: εἰ ἔστι C.   περὶ C   διαιρέσει PJ: διαίρεσις C (an recte?): διαίρεσις B: διαιρέσεις H   7 τῷ Usener   ἀπέχοντος corr. Ross: ἀπέχοντες codd.   9 τἄμφω P: τ' ἄμφω JΣ   10 ἕκαστον Σ

these too must differ, whether the universals are genera or species. Almost all knowledge, too, is of things peculiar to their possessors; for both the substance or essence of each thing is peculiar to it, and the attributes that things are observed to possess of themselves and not incidentally would be found to have been particular attributes belonging to particular things. But in general it is the task of science to grasp what is the same in several things, whether it is asserted of them in common and universally or in some special way with regard to each, e. g. of numbers and lines, of animals and plants; complete science is that which includes both these kinds. But in the case of some things there is a universal end for knowledge (for their cause is found in a universal), while in other cases the individual is the end, viz. in the case of the things in respect of which division can be carried on till the individuals are reached, as in the case of things to be done and things to be made; for it is thus that their actuality exists.

The identical something by means of which we know is identical either in essence or in number or in species or in genus or by analogy, or by any other divisions of identity that there may be besides these; but analogical identity spans the widest interval, as though there were here the greatest distance between the objects, this appearance of distance being due sometimes to ourselves, sometimes to the object, sometimes to both.

'Knowledge' having more than one sense, how is the knowledge of each class of things to be pursued? The starting-point and the chief thing is the appropriate method; e. g. we must distinguish between the first things or objects of reason, and the things

p. 318 Brandisii

καὶ ὑπὸ τὴν φύσιν, αὐτῶν τε τούτων τὰ ἐν ἀρχῇ καὶ ⟨τὰ⟩ ἑπόμενα μέχρι ζῴων καὶ φυτῶν καὶ ἐσχάτων τῶν ἀψύχων. ἔστιν γάρ τι καθ' ἕκαστον γένος ἴδιον, ὥσπερ καὶ ἐν τοῖς μαθηματικοῖς. ἔχει δὲ καὶ αὐτὰ τὰ μαθήματα διαφορὰν καί περ ὁμογενῆ πως ὄντα, διῄρηται δ' ἱκανῶς. εἰ δὲ καὶ ἔνια γνωστὰ τῷ ἄγνωστα εἶναι, καθά πέρ τινές φασιν, ἴδιος ἂν ὁ τρόπος εἴη, διαιρέσεως δέ τινος δεῖται· τάχα δ' ἐφ' ὧν ἐνδέχεται, κατ' ἀναλογίαν οἰκειότερον λέγειν ἢ αὐτῷ τῷ ἀγνώστῳ, καθά περ εἴ τις τῷ ἀοράτῳ τὸ ἀόρατον. πόσοι δ' οὖν τρόποι καὶ ποσαχῶς τὸ εἰδέναι, πειρατέον διελεῖν. ἡ δ' ἀρχὴ πρὸς αὐτὰ ταῦτα καὶ πρῶτον τὸ ἀφορίσαι τί τὸ ἐπίστασθαι. χαλεπώτερον δ' ἂν δόξειεν (οὐ γὰρ οἷόν τε καθόλου καὶ κοινόν τι λαβεῖν ἐν τοῖς πλεοναχῶς λεγομένοις). ᾗ καὶ τοῦτ' ἄπορον ἢ οὐ ῥᾴδιόν γε εἰπεῖν, μέχρι πόσου καὶ τίνων ζητητέον αἰτίας ὁμοίως ἔν τε τοῖς αἰσθητοῖς καὶ νοητοῖς· ἡ γὰρ εἰς τὸ ἄπειρον ὁδὸς ἐν ἀμφοῖν ἀλλοτρία καὶ ἀναιροῦσα τὸ φρονεῖν. ἀρχαὶ δὲ τρόπον τινὰ ἄμφω. τάχα δ' ἡ μὲν ἡμῖν ἡ δ' ἁπλῶς, ἢ τὸ μὲν τέλος ἡ δ' ἡμετέρα τις ἀρχή. μέχρι μὲν οὖν τινὸς δυνάμεθα δι' αἰτίου

9ᵃ 14 τὰ inseruit Wimmer 17 ὁμοιογενῆ Σ 19 γνωτὰ P
22 ἡ Γ: ἦ J 23 ὁρατὸν PJC δ' οὖν] δε J 26 τί supra add. J₁: om. Σ

9ᵇ 1 πολλαχῶς LC ᾗ corr. Ross: ἡ PJ: ἠ cet.: post η lacunam statuit Usener: ἡγούμεθ' οὖν ἐπίστασθαι . . . ci. Usener 2 γε] τε LCΣ 6 ἀρχαί] (-ι ex corr. J): ἀρχας P₁: ἀρχαι corr. P: ἀρχὴ Σ: ἀρχῆς L: ἀρχῆς C ἡμῶν u 7 τῆς αρχηι J

that are movable and fall under the heading of 'nature', and of the latter themselves we must distinguish those that are original and those that follow, right down to animals and plants and finally to inanimate things. For there is something peculiar to each class of things, as in the case of mathematical objects. Even mathematical studies themselves contain a difference, though they are in a sense homogeneous; the distinction is sufficiently familiar. And if there are even certain things that are known by being unknown, as some maintain, the manner of inquiry into them would be one peculiar to them, but needs some care to distinguish it from others; though perhaps, in cases where it is possible, it is more appropriate to describe them by analogy, rather than by the very fact that they are unknown—as if one were to describe the invisible by the mere fact that it is invisible. At all events, we must try to distinguish how many methods there are, and how many kinds of knowledge there are. The starting-point for these problems themselves, and the first thing to be done, is to determine what knowledge is. But this would seem rather difficult (for it is not possible to get anything universal and common in the case of terms that are used in more than one sense); wherefore this also is a question impossible or at any rate not easy to answer, up to what point and of what things we should search for causes, alike in the case of sensible and of intelligible objects; for the infinite regress is in both cases inappropriate and destructive to thought. Both kinds of object are in a sense starting-points. And perhaps we may say that the one is a starting-point for us and the other absolutely, or the one is the end and the other

28 ΘΕΟΦΡΑΣΤΟΥ

p. 318. 319 Brandisii

θεωρεῖν, ἀρχὰς ἀπὸ τῶν αἰσθήσεων λαμβάνοντες·
ὅταν δὲ ἐπ' αὐτὰ τὰ ἄκρα καὶ πρῶτα μεταβαίνωμεν, οὐκέτι δυνάμεθα, εἴτε διὰ τὸ μὴ ἔχειν αἰτίαν εἴτε διὰ τὴν ἡμετέραν ἀσθένειαν ὥσπερ
πρὸς | τὰ φωτεινότατα βλέπειν. τάχα δ' ἐκεῖνο
ἀληθέστερον ὡς αὐτῷ τῷ νῷ τῶν τοιούτων ἡ
θεωρία θιγόντι καὶ οἷον ἀψαμένῳ, διὸ καὶ οὐκ
26 ἔστιν ἀπάτη περὶ αὐτά. Χαλεπὴ δὲ καὶ εἰς αὐτὸ
τοῦθ' ἡ σύνεσις καὶ ἡ πίστις, ἐπεὶ καὶ ἄλλως μέγα
καὶ πρὸς τὰς καθ' ἕκαστα πραγματείας ἀναγκαῖον
καὶ μάλιστα τὰς μεγίστας, ἐν τίνι ποιητέον τὸν
ὅρον, οἷον περὶ τὰς τῆς φύσεως καὶ περὶ τὰς ἔτι
προτέρας. οἱ γὰρ ἁπάντων ζητοῦντες λόγον ἀναιροῦσιν λόγον, ἅμα δὲ καὶ τὸ εἰδέναι· μᾶλλον δ'
ἀληθέστερον εἰπεῖν ὅτι ζητοῦσιν ὧν οὐκ ἔστιν
οὐδὲ πέφυκεν. ὅσοι ⟨δὲ⟩ τὸν οὐρανὸν ἀίδιον ὑπο-
27 λαμβάνουσιν, ἔτι δὲ τὰ κατὰ τὰς φορὰς καὶ τὰ
μεγέθη καὶ τὰ σχήματα καὶ τὰς ἀποστάσεις καὶ
ὅσα ἄλλα ἀστρολογία δείκνυσιν, τούτοις κατά-
λοιπον τά τε πρῶτα κινοῦντα καὶ τὸ τίνος ἕνεκα
λέγειν καὶ τίς ἡ φύσις ἑκάστου καὶ ἡ πρὸς ἄλληλα
θέσις καὶ ἡ τοῦ σύμπαντος οὐσία καὶ ὑποβαίνοντι

9ᵇ 9 λαμβάνονται RB₁HD: λαμβάνοντας u 10 πρῶτον C 13 φωτινότατα J: ποθεινότατα RB₁HD βλέποντες Usener 14 τῶν τοιούτων om. CΣ 15 θιγόντι corr. Brandis: θίγοντι codd. καὶ pr. om. LC 17 ἡ alt. om. LC 19 ἔν τινι JC: ἔν τι RBD: ἐν τι H u 20 οἷον om. u περὶ τὰς pr. corr. Usener: περί τε codd.: περὶ τὴν ci. Usener 21 οἱ] εἰ RB₁HD 22 καὶ om. Σ 24 post πέφυκεν lacunam statuit Usener ὅσοι δὲ corr. Zeller: ὅσοι P: ὅσοι cet.: τοῖς οὖν ci. Usener 25 ἔστι u 27 ἄλλα] ἄλλα ἀπὸ τοῦ C₁: ἄλλα τοῦ corr. C ἀστρολογικὰ δεικνύσιν Usener κατὰ λοιπόν JRD: καταλοιπὸν CBH: κατάλοιπα u

is in a way *our* starting-point. Up to a point, then, we can speculate causally by taking starting-points from our sense-perceptions; but when we pass to the limits and first things themselves, we can no longer do so, whether because they have no cause or owing to our own lack of power to look, as it were, at things of the most dazzling brightness. Perhaps this is a truer way of putting it, that the contemplation of such things is by reason itself, touching and as it were laying its finger on them; wherefore also there is no possibility of deception about them.

Understanding and conviction are difficult at this very point, since apart from its value in other respects it is necessary with a view to particular inquiries, and above all to the most important, to know at what point one should set one's limit; e. g. with regard to inquiries into nature, and those that are even prior to these. For those who demand proof of everything destroy proof, and at the same time knowledge; or rather it is truer to say that they seek proof of things of which there is not and from the nature of the case cannot be proof. But those who suppose the celestial system to be eternal, and besides that hold the views about the movements and sizes and figures and distances, and all the other things that astronomy proves,—for these it remains to specify both the first movers and what they aim at, and what the nature of each of them is and their situation relative to one another, and the substance of the whole, and, coming down the scale, to proceed to the other things in the universe, taking each species or part by itself, until they

10ᵃ 1 τοτε P: τὰ δὲ JC: ταῦτα δὲ τὰ Σ: αὐτὰ δὲ τὰ u   2 λέγει C
3 θέσεις P

p. 319. 320 Brandisii

δὴ πρὸς τὰ ἄλλα καθ' ἕκαστον τῶν εἰδῶν ἢ μερῶν ἄχρι ζῴων καὶ φυτῶν. εἰ οὖν ἀστρολογία συνεργεῖ μέν, οὐκ ἐν τοῖς πρώτοις δὲ τῆς φύσεως, ἕτερα τὰ κυριώτατ' ἂν εἴη καὶ πρότερα· καὶ γὰρ δὴ καὶ ὁ τρόπος, ὡς οἴονταί τινες, οὐ φυσικὸς ἢ οὐ πᾶς. καίτοι τό γε κινεῖσθαι καὶ ἁπλῶς τῆς φύσεως οἰκεῖον καὶ μάλιστα τοῦ οὐρανοῦ. διὸ καὶ εἰ ἐνέργεια τῆς οὐσίας ἑκάστου καὶ τὸ καθ' ἕκαστον ὅταν ἐνεργῇ καὶ κινεῖται, καθά περ ἐν τοῖς ζῴοις καὶ | φυτοῖς (εἰ δὲ μή, ὁμώνυμα), δῆλον ὅτι κἂν ὁ οὐρανὸς ἐν τῇ περιφορᾷ κατὰ τὴν οὐσίαν εἴη, χωριζόμενος δὲ καὶ ἠρεμῶν ὁμώνυμος· οἷον
28 γὰρ ζωή τις ἡ περιφορὰ τοῦ παντός. ἆρ' οὖν εἴ γε μηδ' ἐν τοῖς ζῴοις τὴν ζωὴν ἢ ὡδὶ ζητητέον, οὐδ' ἐν τῷ οὐρανῷ καὶ τοῖς οὐρανίοις τὴν φορὰν ἢ τρόπον τινὰ ἀφωρισμένον; συνάπτει δέ πως ἡ νῦν ἀπορία καὶ πρὸς τὴν ὑπὸ τοῦ ἀκινήτου κίνησιν.

IX Ὑπὲρ δὲ τοῦ πάνθ' ἕνεκά του καὶ μηδὲν μάτην, ἄλλως ⟨θ'⟩ ὁ ἀφορισμὸς οὐ ῥᾴδιος, καθά περ πλεονάκις λέγεται (πόθεν δ' ἄρξασθαι χρὴ καὶ εἰς ποῖα τελευτᾶν;), καὶ δὴ ἔνια τῷ μὴ δοκεῖν ἔχειν οὕτως ἀλλὰ τὰ μὲν συμπτωματικῶς τὰ δ' ἀνάγκῃ τινί, καθά περ ἔν τε τοῖς οὐρανίοις καὶ ἐν τοῖς

10ᵃ 4 τῶν om. J   ἢ μερῶν] ἡμερῶν PJ : ἡμέρων Σ   5 εἰ] ἡ JC ἀστρολόγος R corr. BHD : ἀστρολόγως (ut vid.) R₁   7 τὰ] γὰρ τὰ L : δὲ BH u   κυριώτερα B₁   8 φυσικῶς C₁   10 καὶ εἰ corr. Usener : καὶ ἡ codd. : εἰ ἡ Wimmer   12 κινῆται PJRD   16 ἆρ' O : ἆρ P : ἆρ' cet.   εἴ γε ci. Sylburg : εἴ τε P : εἴ τε cet.   17 μηδὲν τοῖς JC z   ἢ ὡδὶ P : η ωδει JC : om. L : ἢ ᾧ δεῖ cet.   ζητέον P   18 οὐδὲν τῷ J   22 μηδὲν [μάτην] ἄλλως, ὁ ci. Zeller   23 ἄλλως θ' corr. Usener : αλλως P : ἄλλως J : ἀλλ' ὡς CΣ   ἀφωρισμὸς

come down to animals and plants. If then astronomy contributes to our knowledge, but not with regard to the first things in nature, the things that are most dominant must be other than and prior to its objects; for indeed even the method of philosophy, as some think, is not physical, or not the whole of it is so. Yet to be moved is at any rate proper both to nature in general and to the celestial system in particular. Hence also, if activity is of the essence of each natural object, and a particular thing when it is active is also in movement, as in the case of animals and plants (which if they are not in movement are animals and plants only in name), it is clear that the celestial system also in its rotation is in accordance with its essence, and if it were divorced from this and were at rest it would be a celestial system only in name; for the rotation is a sort of life of the universe. Surely, then, if the life in animals does not need 28 explanation or is to be explained only in this way, may it not be the case that in the heavens too, and in the heavenly bodies, movement does not need explanation or is to be explained in a special way? The present problem connects in a way with the imparting of motion by what is unmovable.

With regard to the view that all things are for the IX sake of an end and nothing is in vain, the assignation of ends is in general not easy, as it is usually stated to be (where should we begin and with what sort of things should we finish?), and in particular some things are difficult because they do not seem to be for the sake of an end but to occur, some of them, by coincidence, and others, by some necessity, as in the case both of celestial and of most terrestrial

RBHD corr.   24 τ' ci. Zeller   χρῆν Σ   25 ἔνια τῶν J u: τῷ ἔνια, fortasse recte, vel ἐνίων τῷ ci. Usener

32 ΘΕΟΦΡΑΣΤΟΥ

p. 320. 321 Brandisii

29 περὶ τὴν γῆν πλείοσιν. τίνος γὰρ ἕνεκα αἱ ἔφοδοι καὶ ἀνάρροιαι θαλάττης [ἢ τίνος αἱ προχωρή- 10ᵇ σεις] ἢ ἀναξηράνσεις καὶ ὑγρότητες καὶ ὅλως πρὸς ἄλλοτ' ἄλλο μεταβολαὶ καὶ φθοραὶ καὶ γενέσεις, [ἢ αἱ μὲν ἐν αὐτῇ τῇ γῇ ἀλλοιώσεις καὶ μεταβολαὶ γίνονται πρὸς ἄλλοτ' ἄλλο μεθι- 5 σταμένων] καὶ ἕτερα δ' οὐκ ὀλίγα παρόμοια τούτοις; ἔτι δ' ἐν αὐτοῖς τοῖς ζῴοις τὰ μὲν ὥσπερ μάταια, καθά περ τοῖς ἄρρεσιν οἱ μαστοὶ καὶ τοῖς θήλεσιν ἡ πρόεσις, εἴ περ μὴ συμβάλλεται, καὶ πώγονος δ' ἐνίοις ἢ ὅλως τριχῶν ἔκφυσις ἔν 10 τισιν τόποις· ἔτι δὲ κεράτων μεγέθη καθά περ τῶν ἐλάφων τοῖς ⟨οὐκ ὠφελουμένοις, τοῖς⟩ δὲ καὶ λελωβημέ|νοις κνήσει τε καὶ παραιωρήσει καὶ ἐπιπροσθήσει τῶν ὀμμάτων· καὶ ὡς ἔνια δὴ βίᾳ ἢ παρὰ φύσιν, ὥσπερ ὁ ἐρῳδιὸς ὀχεύει καὶ τὸ ἡμερόβιον ζῇ· 15
30 καὶ ἕτερα οὐκ ὀλίγα λάβοι τις ἂν τοιαῦτα. Καὶ τὸ μέγιστον δὴ καὶ μάλιστα δοκοῦν περὶ τὰς τροφὰς καὶ γενέσεις τῶν ζῴων· οὐθενὸς γὰρ ταῦθ' ἕνεκα, ἀλλὰ συμπτώματα καὶ δι' ἑτέρας ἀνάγκας. ἔδει γάρ, εἴ περ τούτων χάριν, ἀεὶ κατὰ ταὐτὰ καὶ ὡσαύτως. 20 ἔτι δ' ἐν τοῖς φυτοῖς καὶ μᾶλλον τοῖς ἀψύχοις ὡρισμένην τιν' ἔχουσι φύσιν, ὥσπερ δοκοῦσιν, καὶ μορφαῖς καὶ εἴδεσιν καὶ δυνάμεσιν, τίνος ἕνεκα ταῦτα ζητήσειεν ἄν τις. (αὐτὸ γὰρ τοῦτο ἄπορον τὸ

10ᵃ 28 ἕνεκα αἱ εφοδοι P : ἕνεκα αἱ ἔφοδοι J : αἱ ἔφοδοι ἕνεκα Σ
10ᵇ 1 ἢ τίνος αἱ προχωρήσεις seclusit Ross   2 post προχωρήσεις inseruit Usener καὶ ἀναχωρήσεις   ἡ P : ἢ J   3 πρὸ ἄλλοτ' P : αἱ πρὸς ἄλλοτ' L : πρὸς ἄλλο τ' u   4–6 ἢ...μεθισταμένων seclusit Usener   4 τηι supra add. J₁   6 δ' om. Σ   7 ἔστι u   τοῖς om. P   8 μασθοὶ RD   11 ἔτι δὲ] ἔστι δὲ καὶ u   12 τοῖς οὐκ

phenomena. For to what end are the incursions and refluxes of the sea, or droughts and humidities, and, in general, changes, now in this direction and now in that, and ceasings-to-be and comings-to-be, and not a few other things, too, that are like these? Again, in animals themselves some things are practically useless, as for instance in males the breasts and in females the emission peculiar to them, unless indeed this makes some contribution, and in some animals too the growth of a beard or, generally speaking, of hair in certain places; and again the size of the horns, as in deer, for those that are not benefited by them (while some have even been injured by the rubbing of their horns against obstacles or by being suspended by them or by their horns covering up their eyes); and the way in which some phenomena are even violent or unnatural, like the copulation of the heron and the life of the day-fly; and one might find not a few other things of the same kind.

The greatest and most obvious example is in connexion with the nutrition and birth of animals; for there are facts about these which are not for any end, but are coincidences and due to external necessities. For if they were for the sake of the animals, they should have been always uniform and unvaried. Again, in the case of plants and still more of inanimate things that have a nature which is determinate, as it seems, both in respect of shapes and forms and of powers, one might ask what the purpose of these things is. (The very supposition that

ὠφελουμένοις, τοῖς δὲ corr. Ross : τοῖς δὲ codd. : τοῖσδε Usener λελωβημένων PJC, Usener   13 κνήσει corr. Usener: κινήσει codd.   14 δεῖ J : δ' ἡ R   παραφύσειν P   17 μέγιστον] μάλιστα J   20 τούτων] του Usener   ταὐτὰ interpres : ταυτα P : ταῦτα cet.   22 ἔχουσαι PJ   23 εἴδει Σ   τινος J : τίνος γ' Σ

p. 321. 322 Brandisii

μὴ ἔχειν λόγον, καὶ ταῦτ' ἐν ἑτέροις μὴ ποιοῦσιν 25
προτέροις καὶ τιμιωτέροις. ᾗ καὶ ἔοικεν ὁ λόγος
ἔχειν τι πιστόν, ὡς ἄρα τῷ αὐτομάτῳ ταῦτα καὶ τῇ
τοῦ ὅλου περιφορᾷ λαμβάνει τινὰς ἰδέας ἢ πρὸς ἀλ-
λήλα διαφοράς.) εἰ δὲ μή, τοῦ θ' ἕνεκά του καὶ 11ᵃ
εἰς τὸ ἄριστον ληπτέον τινὰς ὅρους καὶ οὐκ ἐπὶ
πάντων ἁπλῶς θετέον· ἐπεὶ καὶ τὰ τοιάδε ἔχει
τινὰ διστασμὸν καὶ ἁπλῶς λεγόμενα καὶ καθ' ἕκα-
στον· ἁπλῶς μὲν ὅτι τὴν φύσιν ⟨εἰκὸς⟩ ἐν ἅπα- 5
σιν ὀρέγεσθαι τοῦ ἀρίστου καὶ ἐφ' ὧν ἐνδέχεται
μεταδιδόναι τοῦ ἀεὶ καὶ τοῦ τεταγμένου· ὡς δ'
αὕτως καὶ ἐπὶ τῶν ζῴων ὁμοίως· ὅπου γὰρ οἷόν
τε τὸ βέλτιον, ἐνταῦθα οὐδαμοῦ παραλείπει, οἷον
τὸ ἔμπροσθεν τὴν φάρυγγα τοῦ οἰσοφάγου (τιμιώ- 10
τερον γάρ), καὶ ἐν | τῇ μέσῃ κοιλίᾳ τῆς καρδίας
τὴν κρᾶσιν ἀρίστην, ὅτι τὸ μέσον τιμιώτατον·
ὡσαύτως δὲ καὶ ὅσα κόσμου χάριν· εἰ γὰρ καὶ
ἡ ὄρεξις οὕτως, ἀλλ' ἐκεῖνό γ' ἐμφαίνει διότι πολὺ
τὸ οὐχ ὑπακοῦον οὐδὲ δεχόμενον τὸ εὖ, μᾶλλον 15
δὲ πολλῷ πλεῖον· ὀλίγον γάρ τι τὸ ἔμψυχον,
ἄπειρον δὲ τὸ ἄψυχον· καὶ αὐτῶν τῶν ἐμψύχων

10ᵇ 25 ποιοῦσιν] προσοῦσαν Usener   26 προτέρως u A   καὶ τιμιωτέροις om. LC   ᾗ corr. Oporinus: ἡ P: ἢ J: ἦ cet.: ἦ u: ἦ ed. Aldina pr.   καὶ om. R   28 ἰδίας corr. J   ἡ P: om. J
11ᵃ 1 διαφοράν L: διαφορὰ C   μή, τοῦ θ' corr. Usener: μὴ τοῦθ' codd., Zeller   τοῦ om. JC   2 ἄριστον, ληπτέον ci. Zeller   καὶ om. Σ   3 τὰ] κατὰ C   4 δυσταγμὸν J: δισταγμὸν C₁Σ   λέγομεν ἃ CΣ   καὶ om. J   καθέκαστον PC: καθ' ἑκάστου Σ   5 ὅτε u εἰκὸς inseruit Usener   ἅπασιν] ἅπασιν ἀνάγκη ci. Usener   8 αὐτὸς P: αὐτὰ JC   ὅποι Σ   9 an παραλείπειν?   10 φάρυγκαν L₁: φάρυγγαν L corr. C   οἰστοφάγου P   12 κρᾶσιν PCΣ   14 an ἐμφαίνεται ὅτι?   πολλὰ C₁   17 ἐμψύχων] ἀψύχων J

they have *no* explanation is difficult, and especially for people who do not make this supposition in the case of other things that are prior and of higher worth. For this reason there seems to be some plausibility in the view that after all it is fortuitously and by the rotation of the universe that these things acquire certain forms or differences from one another.) If they have no purpose, we must set certain limits 31 to purposiveness and to the effort after the best, and not assert it to exist in all cases without qualification; since even statements of the following kind give rise to some doubt, whether they are made without qualification or with reference to particular cases; when it is said without qualification that it is to be expected that nature in all things should desire the best and when it is possible give things a share in the eternal and orderly; and similarly when a corresponding statement is made about animals; for we are told that where the better is possible, there it is never lacking; and this is illustrated by the facts that the windpipe is in front of the gullet (for this is the more honourable position), and that the mixture of the blood is best in the middle ventricle of the heart because the middle is the most honourable part; and similarly with the parts that are for the sake of ornament. For even if 32 this is the desire of nature, still the facts make this at least evident, that there is much that does not obey nor receive the good, or rather that this greatly predominates; for what is animate is a small part of the universe, and what is inanimate is infinite; and of animate things themselves there is only a minute part whose existence is actually better than its nonexistence would be. But to say that *in general* the

p. 322 Brandisii

ἀκαριαίου καὶ βέλτιον τὸ εἶναι. τὸ δ' ὅλον σπάνιόν τι καὶ ἐν ὀλίγοις τὸ ἀγαθόν, πολὺ δὲ πλῆθος εἶναι τὸ κακόν, οὐκ ἐν ἀοριστίᾳ δὲ μόνον καὶ οἷον ὕλης εἴδει, καθά περ τὰ τῆς φύσεως, ἀμαθεστάτου. εἰκῇ γὰρ οἱ περὶ τῆς ὅλης οὐσίας λέγοντες ὥσπερ Σπεύσιππος σπάνιόν τι τὸ τίμιον ποιεῖ τὸ περὶ τὴν τοῦ μέσου χώραν, τὰ δ' ἄκρα καὶ ἑκατέρωθεν. τὰ μὲν οὖν ὄντα καλῶς ἔτυχεν ὄντα.

33 Πλάτων δὲ καὶ οἱ Πυθαγόρειοι μακρὰν τὴν ἀπόστασιν, ἐπιμιμεῖσθαι δ' ἐθέλειν ἅπαντα· καίτοι καθά περ ἀντίθεσίν τινα ποιοῦσιν τῆς ἀορίστου δυάδος καὶ τοῦ ἑνός, ἐν ᾗ καὶ τὸ ἄπειρον καὶ τὸ ἄτακτον καὶ πᾶσα ὡς εἰπεῖν ἀμορφία καθ' αὑτήν, ὅλως οὐχ οἷόν τε ἄνευ ταύτης τὴν τοῦ ὅλου φύσιν, ἀλλ' οἷον ἰσομοιρεῖν ἢ καὶ ὑπερέχειν τῆς ἑτέρας· ᾗ καὶ τὰς ἀρχὰς ἐναντίας. διὸ καὶ οὐδὲ τὸν θεόν, ὅσοι τῷ θεῷ τὴν αἰτίαν ἀνάπτουσιν, δύνασθαι πάντ' εἰς τὸ ἄριστον ἄγειν, ἀλλ' εἴ περ, ἐφ' ὅσον ἐνδέχεται· τάχα δ' οὐδ' ἂν προέλοιτ', εἴ περ ἀναιρεῖσθαι συμβήσεται τὴν ὅλην οὐσίαν ἐξ ἐναν-

11ᵃ 18 ἀκαριαίου καὶ βέλτιον τὸ εἶναι corr. Ross: ἀκαριαῖον καὶ βέλτιον τὸ εἶναι codd.: ἀκαριαῖον καὶ βέλτιον τῷ εἶναι Usener: an ἀκαριαῖον, κεἰ βέλτιον, τὸ εἶναι?   19 τι] τε J corr.m.1 CΣ   20 εἶναι τὸ κακόν u: ἢ τὸ κακόν P: ἢ τὸ κακόν JC: εἰ τὸ κακόν Σ: εἰ τοῦ κακοῦ Usener   οὐκ ἐν corr. Zeller: οὐκ ἢ J: οὐκ εἰ cet.: ἐν Usener   ἀοριστίᾳ corr. Usener: ἀοριστία (ἀριστία R₁) codd.   21 εἴδη P: εἴδη Σ   καθά περ τὰ] καθάπερ τοῦ Vᵃ O: καθαιρεῖν τὰ Usener   ἀμαθέστατον BH u   22 εἰκῇ γὰρ corr. Sylburg: εἰ· καὶ γὰρ P: καὶ γὰρ J: εἰ γὰρ καὶ C: εἰ καὶ γὰρ Σ   23 πεύσιπος J: σπεύσιπος C   24 τὰ δ'] τά τ' ci. Gomperz   25 καὶ delendum ci. Gomperz   ἑκατέρω Σ

11ᵇ 1 ἐπιμιμεῖσθαι δ' ἐθέλειν corr. Ross: ἐπιμμεῖσθαι γ' ἐθέλειν P:

good is something rare and found only in few things, while the evil is a great multitude, and does not consist solely in indefiniteness and exist by way of matter, as *is* the case with the things of nature, is the act of a most ignorant person. For quite random is the talk of those who speak of the whole of reality as Speusippus does when he makes the valuable element to be something scanty, namely, what is found in the region of the centre of the universe, the rest forming the extremes and being to each side of the centre. Rather, reality in fact is and always has been good.

Plato and the Pythagoreans make the distance 33 between the real and the things of nature a great one, but hold that all things wish to imitate the real; yet since they make a sort of opposition between the One and the indefinite dyad, on which essentially depends what is indefinite and disordered and, so to speak, all shapelessness, it is absolutely impossible that for them the nature of the whole should exist without the indefinite dyad; they say that it has an equal share in things with, or even predominates over, the other principle; whereby they make even the first principles contrary to one another. Hence those who ascribe causation to God hold that even God cannot guide everything to what is best; but that if He does so at all, it is only so far as is possible; and presumably He would not even choose to do so, if it is to result in the destruction of the

---

ἐπιμιμεῖσθαι γε θέλειν cet.: ἐπι ... μιμεῖσθαί γ᾽ ἐθέλειν Usener: ἐπινοοῦντες τῶν τῇδε ἀποφαίνονται τὸ ἐν μιμεῖσθαί γ᾽ ἐθέλειν ci. Usener: ἐπινοήσαντες τῶν ἀρχῶν οἴονται τὸ ἐν μιμεῖσθαί γ᾽ ἐθέλειν ci. Diels
5 ὅλως] ὅλως P: ὅλως δ᾽ JCRD: ὅλως δὲ BH: ὡς Usener ἄν ἐν P₁: ἄνευ corr. P₁ 7 ᾗ corr. Ross: ἡ codd. 9 ἀόριστον Σ 11 οὐσίαν] ἁγίαν Σ

ΘΕΟΦΡΑΣΤΟΥ

p. 322. 323 Brandisii

34 τίων γε καὶ ⟨ἐν⟩ ἐναντίοις οὖσαν. φαίνεται δὲ καὶ ἐν | τοῖς πρώτοις ἐπιθεωρούμενα πολλὰ καὶ ὡς ἔτυχεν, οἷον τὰ περὶ τὰς τῆς γῆς λεχθέντα μεταβολάς· οὔτε γὰρ τὸ βέλτιον οὔτε τὸ τινὸς χάριν, ἀλλ' εἴ περ, ἀνάγκῃ τινὶ κατακολουθεῖν· πολλὰ δὲ καὶ ἐν τῷ ἀέρι τοιαῦτα καὶ ἐν ἄλλοις. μάλιστα δ' ἂν δόξειεν ἔχειν τήν γε τάξιν τῶν μὲν αἰσθητῶν τὰ οὐράνια, τῶν δ' ἄλλων, εἰ μὴ ἄρα καὶ πρότερα τούτων, τὰ μαθηματικά· εἰ γὰρ καὶ μὴ πᾶν ἀλλ' ἐν τούτοις πλέον τὸ τεταγμένον. πλὴν εἴ τις τοιαύτας λαμβάνοι τὰς μορφάς οἵας Δημόκριτος ὑποτίθεται τῶν ἀτόμων.

Ἀλλὰ δὴ τούτων μὲν πέρι σκεπτέον· ὃ δ' ἐξ ἀρχῆς ἐλέχθη, πειρατέον τινὰ λαμβάνειν ὅρον καὶ ἐν τῇ φύσει καὶ ἐν τῇ τοῦ σύμπαντος οὐσίᾳ καὶ τοῦ ἕνεκά του καὶ τῆς εἰς τὸ βέλτιον ὁρμῆς. αὕτη γὰρ ἀρχὴ τῆς τοῦ σύμπαντος θεωρίας, ἐν τίσιν τὰ ὄντα καὶ πῶς ἔχει πρὸς ἄλληλα.

Τοῦτο τὸ βιβλίον Ἀνδρόνικος μὲν καὶ Ἕρμιππος ἀγνοοῦσιν, οὐδὲ γὰρ μνείαν αὐτοῦ ὅλως πεποίηνται ἐν τῇ ἀναγραφῇ τῶν Θεοφράστου βιβλίων· Νικόλαος δὲ ἐν τῇ θεωρίᾳ τῶν Ἀριστοτέλους Μετὰ τὰ φυσικὰ μνημονεύει αὐτοῦ, λέγων εἶναι Θεοφράστου. εἰσὶ δ' ἐν αὐτῷ οἷον προδιαπορίαι τινὲς ὀλίγαι τῆς ὅλης πραγματείας.

11b 12 ἐν Β rec., Sylburg: om. cet.   14 τὰ περὶ τὰς Vᵃ corr. O: τὰ περί τε PC: τὰ περί τε τὴν J: τὰ περὶ Vᵃ₁Β u: τὸ περὶ cet.   μεταβολὴν JC   15 τῷ βελτίονι οὔτε τῷ ci. Usener   τίνος R   18 γε corr. Ross: τε PJC: om. cet.   post τάξιν notavit Usener hiatum, intercidisse arbitratus καὶ τὸ ὡρισμένον   20 τούτων] τόπον u   22 λαμβάνει JC u   25 λαβεῖν J   26 παντὸς C
12ᵃ 3 Subscriptionem praebent codices PH :—θεοφράστου τῶν

whole of reality, since this consists of contraries and depends on contraries. Even among first things we evidently observe many events that happen at random, e.g. the facts that have been named, connected with the changes of the earth ; for we see here neither the better nor that which is for the sake of an end, but such things seem to follow, if anything, some necessary law; and there are many things of this sort in the air too, and elsewhere. And it would seem that of sensible things the heavenly bodies possess order, at least, in the highest degree, and of other things the objects of mathematics (unless indeed these are even prior to the heavenly bodies in this respect); for in these if the ordered is not everything, still it is the greater part. Unless indeed one were to take the shapes to be such as those that Democritus ascribes to the atoms.

But at any rate these are the questions we must inquire into. But, as was said at the beginning, we must try to find a certain limit, both in nature and in the reality of the universe, both to final causation and to the impulse to the better. For this is the beginning of the inquiry about the universe, i.e. of the effort to determine the conditions on which real things depend and the relations in which they stand to one another.

μετα τα φυσικά P : θεοφράστου· τῶν μετὰ τὰ φυσικὰ. τέλος H
Subscriptionem alteram praebent codices PRBH :—τὸ om. P
12^b 4 οἷον om. RBH   προδιαπορήσεις RBH

COMMENTARY

Ch. I. The nature of the relation between the first principles and sensible things.
II. Problems about the impulse of sensible things towards the first principle.
III. The importance of deducing the observed facts from the first principles.
IV. Are the first principles definite or indefinite?
V. The supposed immobility of the first principles.
VI. Matter and form.
VII. Good and evil.
VIII. The multiplicity of being and of knowledge.
IX. The limits of teleological explanation.

τινές refers especially to Plato and the Platonists; cf. the 4ᵃ 4 intimation in *Tim.* 59 c d that the study of nature cannot be exact. But there may be also a reference to Aristotle; cf. *Met.* 1026ᵃ 13–16 ἡ μὲν γὰρ φυσικὴ περὶ χωριστὰ μὲν ἀλλ' οὐκ ἀκίνητα . . . ἡ δὲ πρώτη καὶ περὶ χωριστὰ καὶ ἀκίνητα.

μεταβολὰς ἔχουσα παντοίας . . . ἀεὶ κατὰ ταὐτά. There is probably 5–6 some confusion between natural science and its subject-matter. T. speaks as if not only the subject-matter of natural science, but, in consequence, natural science itself, were subject to change.

εὐλογώτερον . . . φθαρτῶν. The suggestion that there ought to 13–16 be some connexion between the different orders of things in the universe is probably inspired by such passages of Aristotle as *H. A.* 588ᵇ 4, *Met.* 1076ᵃ 1, 1090ᵇ 19. The word ἐπεισοδιώδης occurs in the latter two passages.

εἰ μέν is correlative to εἰ δ' ᵇ 6, while εἰ δὲ μή ᵇ 1 is opposed to 18 οἷον γάρ ᵃ 21.

εἰ μὲν γὰρ ἐν τοῖς μαθηματικοῖς μόνον τὰ νοητά. The reference might be either to the theory of Speusippus, which denied the existence of Ideas and treated mathematical objects as the primary realities (Arist. *Met.* 1028ᵇ 21–4, 1076ᵃ 21 f., &c.), or to that of Xenocrates, which identified Ideas with mathematical objects (ib. 1076ᵃ 20 f., &c.); and perhaps both are referred to.

42 COMMENTARY

4ᵃ 20 οὖθ' ὅλως ἀξιόχρεα φαίνεται παντός. Usener proposes αἰτιά τινος for παντός, and πάντως might also be suggested. But ἀξιόχρεως occurs with a genitive in the sense of 'adequate to'; cf. Dem. 8. 49 ἀξιόχρεως τηλικούτου πράγματος, 19. 131 τοσούτων ἀξιόχρεων, and this meaning seems suitable here.

4ᵇ 2 The manuscript reading οὐχ ὥστε συνάπτειν is not impossible, but the double ὥστε would be very awkward, and Usener's οὐχ οὕτως γε συνάπτειν is almost certainly right.

6 εἰ δ' ἑτέρα τις οὐσία προτέρα καὶ κρείττων ἐστίν refers to the view of Plato, which treated the Ideas as prior to the objects of mathematics (Arist. *Met.* 987ᵇ 14–18, 1076ᵃ 19 f., &c.).

9 ἐχούσας, the reading of the better manuscripts, should probably be preferred to ἔχουσαν, the presence of which in the other manuscripts is due simply to emendation. ἔχουσαν would be more correct, but in the careless style of this work ἐχούσας may be explained by the fact that the writer has just suggested (l. 8) that the ἀρχή may be only generically or specifically one, and numerically more than one (cf. l. 11).

5ᵃ 2 ἡ τοῦ ὀρεκτοῦ φύσις. The reference is to Aristotle's doctrine that the prime mover moves the celestial spheres (and incidentally terrestrial things) by being an object of desire. Cf. *Phys.* viii. 5, 6, *De An.* iii. 10, *Met.* Λ. 6, 7 (esp. 1072ᵃ 26).

3 In view of ᵇ 23 it seems as if ἡ κυκλική had become almost a technical term in the sense of ἡ κυκλικὴ κίνησις, so that the insertion of κίνησις is unnecessary.

ἅπαντος apparently does not occur elsewhere in any classical author, and it seems unsafe to introduce it into the text (as Usener does) on the strength of P alone. P is careless in such matters; cf. 9ᵃ 19 γνωτά ... ἄγνωστα, 22 ἀγνώστῳ, 7ᵃ 3 συνακολουσθεῖ, ᵇ 3 ἑστησίους.

4 κατ' ἐκεῖνο, i. e. τὸ ὀρεκτόν (l. 2).

τὸ μὴ εἶναι κινήσεως ἀρχὴν ἢ εἰ κινούμενον κινήσει, lit. 'the statement that there is no starting-point of motion, or that there is one only if a thing is to initiate motion by being moved itself'. Thus the meaning comes to be the same as if πλήν had stood in place of ἤ. Cf. Arist. *Met.* 1084ᵇ 33 οὐθενὶ γὰρ διαφέρει ἢ ὅτι ἀρχή, and Kühner, *Gr. Gramm.* ii. 2. § 540, Anm. 4. The construction is a favourite one with T.; cf. 7ᵇ 8, 10ᵃ 17, 19.

The reference is to Plato's doctrine that the κινήσεως ἀρχή is

τὸ αὐτὸ κινοῦν. Cf. *Phaedr.* 245, *Laws* 896 a, and Arist. *De An.* 5ª 4
406ᵇ 26 on the doctrine of the *Timaeus*. The same doctrine is
assigned to the Atomists and the Pythagoreans in *De An.* 403ᵇ
28–404ª 20. Aët. iv. 2. 2 says that Alcmaeon (whose views were
akin to those of the Pythagoreans, Arist. *Met.* 986ª 27–31) described
the soul as a φύσις αὐτοκίνητος.

οὕτω ... ἀπόφασις. The meaning seems to be that it is better 10–13
to say that the πρώτη ἀρχή belongs to a class of things which
could not be divisible into parts than to put it into a class (that
of material things) which would naturally be divisible, and then
deny divisibility of it.

ἅμᾳ. P reads ἅμαι here, ἅμαι in 5ª 25, ᵇ 3, 6ª 8, ᵇ 3, ἅμα in 12
9ᵇ 22. ἁμᾷ or ἁμᾶ occurs in Pind. *Ol.* 3. 21, *Pyth.* 3. 36, Ar.
Lys. 1318, Call. *Lav. Pall.* 75, Theoc. 9. 4, and is recognized by
Herodian Grammaticus (i. 489 Lentz). The word would seem to
have been originally a locative, and it seems quite likely that P
has preserved Theophrastus' actual way of writing it.

T. now turns from the good points of Aristotle's doctrine of the 14
first mover (stated in ll. 5–13) to point out difficulties in the
theory.

πλείω ... ὑπεναντίαι refers especially to ποία, 17 καὶ τὸ ἀνήνυτον 15–16
... ἀφανές to τίνων.

αἱ φοραὶ τρόπον τινὰ ὑπεναντίαι. Aristotle's theory, stated in 16
Met. Λ. 8, involved: (1) movements of spheres in the plane of
the equator, (2) movements in the plane of the ecliptic, (3) movements across the breadth of the zodiac, (4) movements in a plane
perpendicular to the ecliptic, (5) movements oblique to movements (4), and (6) movements in the reverse direction to all those
previously mentioned except (1). T. is justified in asking how
all of these can be produced by desire for a single prime mover.
According to Aristotle all the movements except (1) are directly
due to the influence of subordinate agents (the 'intelligences' of
the schoolmen); but the relation of these to the prime mover
remains very obscure. Cf. Arist. *Met.*, ed. Ross, I. cxxxv–cxli.

ὥστε. Most of the instances of ὥστε in apodosi quoted in 20
Bonitz's *Index Aristotelicus* 873ª 31–44 are in longish sentences,
in which the intervening clauses make the construction less sur-
prising. But there is at any rate one instance of it in a sentence
in which the protasis is quite short, viz. *Phys.* 232ª 12–14 εἰ οὖν

44 COMMENTARY

5ᵃ 20 ἀνάγκη ἢ ἠρεμεῖν ἢ κινεῖσθαι πᾶν, ἠρεμεῖ δὲ καθ' ἕκαστον τῶν ΑΒΓ, ὥστ' ἔσται τι συνεχῶς ἠρεμοῦν ἅμα καὶ κινούμενον.

23 ὅ γε τῶν ἀστρολόγων, i. e. the theory accepted by Aristotle in *Met.* Λ. 8, but only provisionally, in order to have some theory to account for the facts (ἐννοίας χάριν ... ὅπως ᾖ τι τῇ διανοίᾳ πλῆθος ὡρισμένον ὑπολαβεῖν, 1073ᵇ 12 f.).

25-8 τί ... ἕν. T. turns aside from his criticism of Aristotle's explanation of the movements in the universe to make a similar criticism of the Academy's explanation of the sensible world by derivation from the One or from numbers. The point of similarity is that, whether we say that the sensible world 'desires' or that it 'imitates' the first principle, we should expect to find it in that case having the same characteristics as the first principle—not movement but rest, not disorder, which the Platonists ascribe to the sensible world (cf. 4ᵃ 4), but order such as they ascribe to the intelligible first principles; cf. 4ᵃ 6.

25 τί οὖν ἅμα τῇ μιμήσει φασὶν ἐκεῖνο. Usener interprets ἐκεῖνο as = τὸ φυσικὴν ὄρεξιν ἔχοντα κινεῖσθαι. Then the meaning will be: 'why do those who maintain the primacy of the One or of the numbers combine the assertion that sensible things have a desire towards the first mover, with the assertion that sensible things imitate the One and the numbers?' There are two fatal objections, as it seems, to this interpretation: (1) It was not the same thinkers that held the doctrine of ὄρεξις for the first mover, and the doctrine that sensible things imitate the One or the numbers. The first is the view of Aristotle, the second that of the Pythagoreans and Plato. (2) If the point were the combination of the doctrine of ὄρεξις with that of μίμησις in the minds of the same thinkers, the objection would have no force unless there were some conflict between the two theories. But obviously these two theories agree in the point on which T. is concentrating: whether you describe sensible things as desiring or as imitating the first principles, this desire or imitation might be expected to produce likeness, and not the unlikeness which actually exists, between their characteristics and those of the first principles.

It appears, therefore, that a different interpretation is needed. ἐκεῖνο must refer simply to τὴν κίνησιν. The objection T. makes to the Platonists is that they have no right to combine the doctrine that sensible things are in movement with the doctrine that sensible things imitate the One or the numbers; for these 5ᵃ 25 are certainly not in movement.

If it be asked, why not ἐκείνην, the answer is that T. tends to revert to the neuter when he is referring to anything inanimate. Cf. 6ᵇ 17 τούτοις referring to τῶν ἀρχῶν, l. 16; 6ᵇ 19 ἐκείνοις referring to ταῖς ἄλλαις μεθόδοις, l. 18.

The omission of ὁμοίως in P seems to be due to haplography. The construction is Theophrastean; cf. 9ᵇ 3 ὁμοίως ἔν τε τοῖς αἰσθητοῖς καὶ νοητοῖς.

ὅσοι τε τὸ ἓν καὶ ὅσοι τοὺς ἀριθμοὺς λέγουσιν. The general 26 reference is to the Pythagorean and Platonic derivation of the sensible world from the One and from numbers. T. seems to distinguish between some who emphasized the One and others who emphasized the numbers. Some light may be thrown on this by Arist. *Met.* 1085ᵃ 13, where Aristotle says that as regards the formal principle involved in geometrical objects different Platonists held different views, and Ps.-Alexander (*in Met.* 777. 17) interprets this as meaning that some of them thought that the ideal numbers were the forms of geometrical objects, while others thought that the One was their form. Both views are suggested in *Met.* 1001ᵇ 24 οὔτε γὰρ ὅπως ἐξ ἑνὸς καὶ ταύτης (*sc.* inequality) οὔτε ὅπως ἐξ ἀριθμοῦ τινὸς καὶ ταύτης γένοιτ' ἂν τὰ μεγέθη, δῆλον. Alexander may well preserve a genuine tradition in holding that different Platonists held the two different views, and if so, it was probably Xenocrates that derived geometrical objects from numbers. For the evidence cf. Ross on *Met.* 1085ᵃ 13-14. We do not know who it was that held the other view, deriving geometrical objects directly from the One.

καὶ γὰρ αὐτοὶ τοὺς ἀριθμούς φασιν τὸ ἕν. T. cannot be saying 27 that these thinkers identified the numbers and the One; the statement would be irrelevant, and would be not only obviously untrue in itself, but quite impossible when T. has just distinguished those who derived things from the One and those who derived them from the numbers. It seems that from μιμήσει, l. 25, we should understand here μιμεῖσθαι, with τοὺς ἀριθμούς as subject and τὸ ἕν as object. Then the clause describes an intelligible theory; and it is pertinent for T. to point out that even those who did not speak of the imitation of the One by all things, but spoke of numbers as the true reality, still introduced imitation of

5ª 27 the One into their theory, since they described the numbers as themselves imitating the One. The theory was in fact that, as the numbers are the formal principle in material things, the One is the formal principle in the numbers. Cf. Arist. *Met.* 987ᵇ 21, 988ᵇ 2, 1080ᵇ 6. For similar ellipses cf. 6ᵇ 3 χρόνον δ' ἅμα καὶ οὐρανὸν καὶ ἕτερα δὴ πλείω, where γεννῶσι has to be 'understood' from γεννήσαντες, 6ª 25, six lines back; 6ᵇ 16 ἔνιοι δὲ καὶ τὴν ἀλήθειαν ἐν τούτοις, *sc.* τιθέασι, or εἶναί φασι; 6ᵇ 25 ὥσπερ ὅσοι πῦρ καὶ γῆν, *sc.* ἀρχὰς ποιοῦσι ; 8ª 2 τί γὰρ αὐτοῖς οὐ συνακολουθεῖ ἡ τῶν ἄλλων (*sc.* ἠρεμία) ; 10ª 25 καὶ δὴ ἔνια (*sc.* οὐ ῥᾴδιά ἐστιν ἀφορίζεσθαι).

28–ᵇ 2 εἰ ... κινούμενα. This seems to be no mere dialectical objection, but to represent T.'s real view; for Proclus says of him (*in Tim.* 35 a = ii. 122. 11 Diehl) ἔμψυχον γὰρ καὶ αὐτὸς εἶναι δίδωσι τὸν οὐρανὸν καὶ διὰ τοῦτο θεῖον· εἰ γὰρ θεῖός ἐστι, φησί, καὶ τὴν ἀρίστην ἔχει διαγωγήν, ἔμψυχός ἐστιν· οὐδὲν γὰρ τίμιον ἄνευ ψυχῆς, ὡς ἐν τῇ περὶ Οὐρανοῦ γέγραφεν.

5ᵇ 3 ψυχῇ δ' ἅμα δοκεῖ καὶ κίνησις ὑπάρχειν. T.'s objection is this. Aristotle's system explains the movement of the heavenly bodies (and ultimately terrestrial movement as well) by their impulse towards the first mover. But if this 'impulse' is to be taken seriously, it implies that the heavenly bodies have soul; and if they have soul, they already have movement—not in the literal sense, but in that of psychical change (ἡ τῆς ψυχῆς, l. 8); so that what is put forward as the cause of movement presupposes the existence of movement. And, further, while the best thing in the world might be expected to produce the best kind of movement, the spatial movement produced by the first mover is inferior to the psychical movement which the spatial movement presupposes (cf. ll. 7–10, 26–8).

ζωὴ γὰρ τοῖς ἔχουσιν, ἀφ' ἧς καὶ αἱ ὀρέξεις πρὸς ἕκαστον, ὥσπερ καὶ τοῖς ζῴοις. Two points are doubtful here: (1) whether ψυχή or κίνησις is to be understood as the subject of the clause ζωὴ γὰρ τοῖς ἔχουσιν, and (2) whether the antecedent of ἧς is (*a*) ζωή, or (*b*) κίνησις (which would involve treating either ζωὴ γὰρ τοῖς ἔχουσιν, or ζωὴ γάρ, as parenthetical), or (*c*) ψυχῇ. But (1) if we are right in our interpretation of the previous clause, the subject of ζωὴ γὰρ τοῖς ἔχουσιν must be ψυχή. The argument is : soul brings with it movement ; for it is life to its possessors (and life

evidently involves movement in some sense, i. e. at least psychical 5ᵇ 3
change). Question (2) is harder to answer. ψυχῇ is too remote
to be easily treated as the antecedent of ἧς. κίνησις might be
treated as the antecedent; and in l. 10 desire is actually said to
proceed from the movement of thought. But the point made in
what immediately follows the words we are considering (i. e. in
ll. 5–7) is that even perception (and therefore *a fortiori* desire,
which presupposes perception) presupposes soul. This follows
more naturally if ζωή rather than κίνησις is the antecedent of ἧς;
for, soul being simply the principle of life, it is very much the
same to say that desires spring from life as it would be to say that
they spring from soul.

The manuscript reading ἔμψυχοι can hardly be right, and a 6
better contrast with καίπερ ἐν τῷ (*sc.* τὸ σῶμα) πάσχειν οὖσαι δι'
ἑτέρων is got by reading ἐν ψυχῇ than by reading ἐμψύχοις. ἐν
ψυχῇ would easily be corrupted by itacism into ἔμψυχοι.

τῶν δὲ περὶ τὸ μέσον οὐθέν. Aristotle (who is being criticized) 12
would not have admitted that in his system terrestrial things are
not ἐφετικὰ τοῦ πρώτου κινοῦντος. For the cyclical transmutation
of the elements, and the never-failing succession of the genera-
tions of living things, are represented by him as being the best
that terrestrial things can attain in their attempt to imitate the
eternal life of God. But it is an undeniable flaw in his system
that, while he describes the heavenly spheres as imitating this
eternal life by eternal rotation, he ascribes to the terrestrial
elements an entirely different movement, movement up or down
in straight lines. It is this that T. has in mind.

αὐτῇ . . . θαλάσσῃ. *Il.* viii. 24. Arist. *De Motu An.* 699ᵇ 37– 17
700ᵃ 2 quotes verses 21–2, 20 in a similar context dealing with
the first mover.

ἀσύνετον, Usener's conjecture, is probably right; cf. l. 9 ἡ τῆς 18
διανοίας (*sc.* κίνησις), ἀφ' ἧς καὶ ἡ ὄρεξις.

ἡ κυκλική. Cf. ᵃ 3 n. 23

λαμβάνει, Usener's conjecture, is almost certainly right. With
this word substituted for συμβαίνει, which gives an impossible
construction, we get a clause (as Usener points out) very like
10ᵇ 27–11ᵃ 1 τῷ αὐτομάτῳ ταῦτα καὶ τῇ τοῦ ὅλου περιφορᾷ λαμβάνει
τινὰς ἰδέας ἢ πρὸς ἄλληλα διαφοράς.

Εἰ . . . βουλόμενον. T. now reverts from the objection he raises 26–6ᵃ 2

48 COMMENTARY

5ᵇ 26– 6ᵃ 2
with regard to terrestrial things to the objection already raised in ll. 7–10 with regard to the heavenly bodies. Thus ll. 10–26 are to some extent parenthetical. But, as has been pointed out in our introduction (p. xix), they contain some points which are taken up in the section beginning at l. 26.

5ᵇ 27
κάλλιον ἄν τι παρὰ τοῦ πρώτου δέοι τῆς κυκλοφορίας. Some word like γίνεσθαι must be supplied in thought, as with such phrases as εἴ τι δέοι.

6ᵃ 1
τὸ γὰρ δὴ πρῶτον καὶ θειότατον πάντα τὰ ἄριστα βουλόμενον. This is curiously inconsequent; for from 5ᵃ 14 onwards T. has been criticizing the theology of Aristotle, but Aristotle does not ascribe to his first mover a wish for what is best. He describes the life of the first mover as one of pure self-contemplation, in which there is no place for βούλησις. Indeed this feature of the divine life is characteristic not of Aristotle's system at all but of Plato's. It may be, however, that T. has in mind not the explicit account of the divine life in *Met.* Λ. 9, but occasional passages in which a doctrine of divine providence is suggested, such as *De Caelo* 271ᵃ 33, *De Gen. et Corr.* 336ᵇ 31, *Met.* 984ᵇ 15, 1075ᵃ 15, 19, 1076ᵃ 4.

4
ἅπανθ' ὅμοια καὶ ἐν τοῖς ἀρίστοις εἶναι. This might be rendered 'that all things should be alike, even among the things that are best'. But a comparison with 8ᵇ 1 ὅ τι οὐ πάντ' ἀγαθὰ οὐδὲ πάντα ὅμοια shows that the meaning is 'that all things should be alike and of the best'.

14
Καὶ τοῦτο μὲν ὥσπερ ἑτέρων λόγων. T. feels that in raising the difficulty he has raised in ll. 5–14, whether movement is of the essence of the sphere of the fixed stars, he is departing too far from his main subject, the nature of the first principles of the universe—in fact, passing from metaphysics to astronomy. He reverts, therefore, to the importance of not merely putting forward certain first principles (as most thinkers have done), but verifying their validity by deducing from them the actual contents of the universe.

15–18
The traditional punctuation here is: ἀπὸ δ' οὖν ταύτης ἢ τούτων τῶν ἀρχῶν ἀξιώσειεν ἄν τις. τάχα δὲ καὶ ἀπὸ τῶν ἄλλων ἄρ', ἄν τις τίθηται τὰ ἐφεξῆς εὐθὺς ἀποδιδόναι ... παύεσθαι. Here ἀξιώσειεν has no object, and the ἄν clause is untranslatable; both defects are remedied (as Zeller pointed out) by abolishing the full stop after τις and treating τάχα ... τίθηται as parenthetical.

ἄρ' is rather lacking in point, and ἇς ἄν τις τίθηται (the reading, 6ᵃ 17 apparently, of a later hand in J) may be the true reading.

All that is known of Eurytus is given in Diels, *Vors.*³ i. 302. 8, 19–22 16–19, 320. 19–321. 17. He is named as a pupil of Philolaus by Iamblichus (*V. P.* 139, 148), who describes him as a native of Croton (ib. 148), or of Tarentum (ib. 267, with which Diog. Laert. viii. 46 and Apuleius, *Dogm. Plat.* 3 agree); and as living later at Metapontium (ib. 266). Diogenes (iii. 6) and Apuleius (l. c.) name him among the Italian teachers of Plato. He is probably identical with the Eurysus from whom Stobaeus (*Anth.* i. p. 89. 25 W.) and Clement (*Strom.* v. 29 = ii. 344. 21 Stählin) quote spurious fragments. Diogenes (viii. 46) describes the last of the Pythagoreans—Xenophilus, Phanton, Echecrates (familiar in Plato's *Phaedo* and ninth letter), Diocles, and Polymnastus—as pupils of Philolaus and Eurytus. Eurytus' floruit may be dated about 400 B.C.

T.'s account of him simply summarizes what Aristotle says of him in *Met.* 1092ᵇ 8–13. Ps.-Alexander *in Met.* 827. 9–26 gives a little further information. It seems, from what Aristotle and ps.-Alexander say, that he carried further the usual Pythagorean method of representing numbers by suitable geometrical forms. They represented numbers of the type 3, 6, 10 ... as triangles—

∴   ∴·∴   ∴∴∴∴ , &c.

numbers of the type 4, 9, 16 ... as squares—

∷   ∷∷∷   ∷∷∷∷ , &c.,

and similarly with numbers of more complicated types. Eurytus conceived the notion that there was similarly a geometrical figure by which the shape typical of each animal or vegetable species could be represented, and made diagrams of them by sticking pebbles in lime. The number of man, then, was the number of pebbles required to represent the human figure, and so with each other species. The procedure was a naïve one, and there is probably some irony in T.'s approval of it.

The passage in Aristotle's *Metaphysics* does not refer to Archytas, and T.'s knowledge that Archytas described Eurytus' method may have come from the separate work which Aristotle wrote on the philosophy of Archytas (cf. Diels, ib. 326. 4–9).

6ª 24 οἱ τὸ ἓν καὶ τὴν ἀόριστον δυάδα ποιοῦντες. It has been doubted whether Plato used the phrase ἀόριστος δυάς, and Heinze maintains that the phrase originated with Xenocrates. But though Aristotle never in so many words ascribes it to Plato, his language strongly suggests that Plato used it as an equivalent for τὸ μέγα καὶ (τὸ) μικρόν, which he undoubtedly used to describe the material principle which co-operated with the One in producing the numbers and, indirectly, material things. This is confirmed by 11ª 27–ᵇ 3 of the present work, and by statements by the Platonist Hermodorus (ap. Simpl.), Alexander, Simplicius, Syrianus, and Asclepius. The best discussion of the subject is in Robin, *La Théorie Platonicienne des Idées et des Nombres*, 641–54, and a brief discussion will be found in Ross, *Arist. Met.* 1081ª 14 n.

It would seem, then, that ἀόριστος δυάς was a phrase used by Plato in his later years for the 'great and small' or indefinite quantity which we find already referred to in the *Philebus* (23 c–25 d) as the ἀπειρία involved in all οὐσία.

25 τοὺς γὰρ ἀριθμοὺς γεννήσαντες. The numbers were, in the Platonic system, the first products of the One and the indefinite dyad. They were supposed to be produced by successive fixations of the indefinite increase and diminution of indefinite quantity, by the application of the One, which was the principle of form and definiteness. The precise mode of the generation of the numbers is a very difficult question, and one too complicated to be discussed here; we may refer to the discussion in Ross, *Arist. Met.* I. lvii–lxiv, and to the fuller discussion by Robin there summarized and criticized.

A very ingenious suggestion has been made by Prof. A. E. Taylor as to the precise meaning of the generation of numbers by the One and the indefinite dyad (*Mind*, 1926, 419–40 and 1927, 12–33). The suggestion, briefly stated, is as follows: Greek mathematicians were interested in the problem of finding approximations to the value of irrational roots, and devised, probably as early as the time of Plato, the following method of approximating to the length of the diagonal of a square in terms of the side (i.e. to the value of $\sqrt{2}$). They set out a column of side-numbers (πλευρικοὶ ἀριθμοί) and a column of corresponding diagonal-numbers (διαμετρικοὶ ἀριθμοί). The first number in each was 1. Each

COMMENTARY 51

subsequent side-number was formed by adding to the previous 6ª 25
side-number the corresponding diagonal-number; each subsequent diagonal-number was formed by adding to the previous diagonal-number twice the corresponding side-number. Thus we get

Side-numbers.	Diagonal-numbers.
1	1
2	3
5	7
12	17
29	41
70	99

and so on. It can be easily verified that $\frac{1}{1}, \frac{3}{2}, \frac{7}{5}, \frac{17}{12}, \frac{41}{29}, \frac{99}{70}$ are successively closer approximations to the value of $\sqrt{2}$, and that they are alternately less and greater than it; and it can be shown without much difficulty that this method is bound always to yield closer and closer approximations, alternately less and greater than $\sqrt{2}$.

This method of approximation to the length of the diagonal of a square in terms of the side is given in Theo Smyrnaeus (42-5 Hiller), and the phrases πλευρικοὶ ἀριθμοί and διαμετρικοὶ ἀριθμοί, which do not occur there, are found in *Theolog. Arithm.* 3 Ast. The proof of the validity of the method is given in Proclus *in Rempubl.* (Kroll ii. 24-6, 27-9; ib., Excursus ii, pp. 393-400).

This method of evaluation of numbers, by fixing alternately an upper and a lower limit to their value, was, Professor Taylor thinks, what Plato meant by the generation of numbers by the great and the small. But so far we have dealt only with irrational numbers, while the constant testimony of ancient writers is that Plato generated numbers *simpliciter* from the great and the small. Professor Taylor thinks, therefore, that Plato generalized the method originally devised for the evaluation of irrationals, and evaluated rationals also by approximations alternately too great and too small. Thus $\frac{2}{3}$ can be approximated to by the series $1 - \frac{1}{2} + \frac{1}{4} - \frac{1}{8} \ldots$.

This suggestion assigns a more definite meaning to the doctrine of the One and the indefinite dyad than had hitherto been assigned, and is for that reason very attractive. But certain considerations seem to be hostile to it. (1) There is no *conclusive* evidence that the above method of evaluating irrationals was known in Plato's time. The earliest mention of it is in Theo Smyrnaeus, who flourished about A.D. 130. Theo's mathematics is in substance Pythagorean, and he states (pp. 1, 16 Hiller) that his purpose is to supply the mathematical knowledge necessary for the understanding of Plato's works. But it would be unsafe to infer that everything in his book was already known to Plato. Yet it is not improbable that this particular method of evaluating $\sqrt{2}$ was known to Plato. He refers to 7 as the 'rational diagonal' of 5 (*Rep.* 546 c), i.e. as a rational approximation to the value of $5\sqrt{2}$, and as he puts this forward not as a new discovery but, apparently, as a matter of general knowledge, it is not unlikely that he knew the whole method.

But (2) there is no evidence that any Greeks in Plato's time knew of a corresponding method of evaluating other irrational square roots than $\sqrt{2}$, or any cube roots.

(3) Though a corresponding method can be used for approximating to the value of a rational fraction, there is (so far as we know) no evidence that any Greeks used this.

(4) A corresponding method which has been suggested, of approximating to the value of a whole number—viz. that of treating $\frac{2}{1}$, $\frac{1}{2}$, $\frac{3}{2}$, $\frac{2}{3}$, $\frac{4}{3}$, $\frac{3}{4}$ ... as successive approximations to the value of 1—is evidently quite pointless, since in using 1, 2, 3, 4 we have all along assumed that we knew the value of 1 already.

(5) The indefinite dyad of the great and the small is described by Aristotle as being, according to the Platonists, the material principle of *numbers*. Now we have no conclusive evidence that Plato ever meant by numbers anything other than the integers. In *Hipp. Maj.* 303 b irrationals are referred to simply as ἄρρητα. In *Rep.* 534 d we have the phrase 'irrational like *lines*'. In *Rep.* 546 c Plato speaks of rational and irrational diagonals of 5, where the irrational diagonal of 5 is $5\sqrt{2}$ and the rational diagonal is a rational approximation to this, viz. 7. In the *Theaetetus* numbers are divided *exhaustively* into square numbers (τετράγωνοι, ἰσόπλευροι) and non-square whole numbers (προμήκεις, ἑτερομήκεις) (147 e–148 a), and the square roots of these are called not numbers but γραμμαί (148 a), and divided correspondingly into μήκη (rational roots) and δυνάμεις (irrational roots) (147 d, 148 a). In

COMMENTARY 53

Polit. 266 a b we have 'the diagonal which is in square (δυνάμει) 6ᵃ 25 2 feet', i.e. the diagonal of the square with side 1 foot; and 'the diagonal of the diagonal', i.e. the diagonal of the square with side √2 feet. In *Laws* 819 e–820 c it is μῆκος, πλάτος, βάθος that are said to be incommensurable (ἄμετρα). It is only in the *Epinomis*, whose Platonic authorship is doubtful though it can no longer be confidently denied, that we find irrational numbers definitely recognized (ταῦτα δὲ μαθόντι τούτοις ἐφεξῆς ἐστιν ὃ καλοῦσι μὲν σφόδρα γελοῖον ὄνομα γεωμετρίαν, τῶν οὐκ ὄντων δὲ ὁμοίων ἀλλήλοις φύσει ἀριθμῶν ὁμοίωσις πρὸς τὴν τῶν ἐπιπέδων μοῖραν γεγονυῖά ἐστιν διαφανής, 990 d; i.e. the problem of irrationals is to be treated as an arithmetical, not a geometrical one). It is therefore doubtful whether Plato ever spoke of irrational numbers; the question could be settled only if we could be sure that he wrote the *Epinomis*.

(6) Aristotle's references show very plainly that he regarded the indefinite dyad as the material principle held by Plato to be involved in the generation of the integers, and of nothing else. Now the method of alternate approximation from above and below appears to be entirely unusable for this purpose. If we are to accept the proposed theory we shall have to suppose that Plato was so much dominated by 'irrationals' that he put forward as a method for the generation of all numbers a method which he knew (if we admit for the sake of argument that he did know it) for the generation of one particular irrational, viz. √2, but which is unmeaning when applied to the generation of integers.

(7) While apparently no Greek writer suggests a connexion between the Platonic 'great and small' and the side and diagonal numbers, the more general interpretation of the former mentioned at the beginning of our note is given by Aristotle (*Phys.* 206ᵇ 27–9), by the Platonist Hermodorus (ap. Simpl. *in Phys.* 247. 30–248. 18), and by Simplicius himself (ib. 455. 1).

(8) In Professor Taylor's interpretation, though an exact account is offered of the part played by the great and small in the Platonic generation of numbers, the part played by the One, which cannot have been less important, is left somewhat obscure.

On the whole, therefore, while recognizing the great interest of the suggestion, and admitting that τὸ μέγα καὶ τὸ μικρόν would have been a very appropriate way of referring to the method of alternate

6ᵃ 25 approximation, we do not think it very likely that that is what the phrase as used by Plato actually meant.

26 καὶ τὰ ἐπίπεδα καὶ τὰ σώματα. From various references in Arist. *Met.* it seems possible to distinguish three modes in which the Platonic school conceived of the generation of planes and solids. (1) Plato distinguished 'ideal magnitudes', i.e. the essence of the line and of the various plane and solid figures, each of which is unique, from the 'mathematical magnitudes', of each of which there is an indefinite plurality. He generated the ideal magnitudes from the One and from the various species of the 'great and small'. The One was in each case the formal principle; the 'long and short' was the material principle of lines, the 'broad and narrow' that of planes, the 'deep and shallow' that of solids. We may suppose that the three grades of ideal magnitudes, once generated, were treated as formal principles, the application of which to the ἀπειρία of space produced the mathematical magnitudes.

(2) Speusippus rejected the ideal magnitudes, and maintained only the existence of mathematical magnitudes (as well as, of course, sensible magnitudes). He made the point the formal principle, and 'something akin to plurality' the material principle, whereby they were generated.

(3) Xenocrates identified the ideal and the mathematical magnitudes. He agreed with Plato in treating the various species of the great and the small as their material principles. He differed from him in identifying the formal principle not with the One but with various numbers, i.e., he derived lengths from the number 2, planes from 3, solids from 4.

Since T. later distinguishes Speusippus and Xenocrates (ᵇ 6 f.) from the thinkers he is at present speaking of, we may assume that he is now speaking of Plato and his orthodox followers.

28 τὰ μὲν ἀπὸ τῆς ἀορίστου δυάδος, οἷον τόπος καὶ κενὸν καὶ ἄπειρον, τὰ δ' ἀπὸ τῶν ἀριθμῶν καὶ τοῦ ἑνός, οἷον ψυχὴ καὶ ἄλλ' ἄττα. This should be compared with Arist. *Met.* 1084ᵃ 32–6 γεννῶσι γοῦν τὰ ἑπόμενα, οἷον τὸ κενόν, ἀναλογίαν, τὸ περιττόν, τὰ ἄλλα τὰ τοιαῦτα, ἐντὸς τῆς δεκάδος· τὰ μὲν γὰρ ταῖς ἀρχαῖς ἀποδιδόασιν, οἷον κίνησιν στάσιν, ἀγαθὸν κακόν, τὰ δ' ἄλλα τοῖς ἀριθμοῖς.

τόπος, κενόν, and ἄπειρον in T.'s statement are probably alternative ways of referring to Plato's doctrine of χώρα. Similarly,

COMMENTARY 55

Aristotle in *Phys.* 209^b 15 describes Plato as identifying τόπος 6^a 28 and χώρα (cf. *Tim.* 52 b 4 ἔν τινι τόπῳ καὶ κατέχον χώραν τινά). He also says that in the ἄγραφα δόγματα Plato identified τὸ μεθεκτικόν or τόπος with τὸ μέγα καὶ τὸ μικρόν, i. e. with the indefinite dyad (*Phys.* 209^b 13, 35); and further that Plato identified τὰ ἄπειρα with τὸ μέγα καὶ τὸ μικρόν (ib. 203^a 15). Aristotle's references would imply that Plato *identified* τόπος, κενόν, or ἄπειρον with the indefinite dyad, but in a sense T.'s statement that he *derived* them from the indefinite dyad is more correct. For it is clear that according to Plato numbers were more fundamental entities than the spatial magnitudes, and stood nearer to the first principles, the One and the indefinite dyad. The indefinite dyad in its primary form, therefore, is not space but indefinite plurality; and space (which is what T. means by τόπος, κενόν, and ἄπειρον) must have been regarded as a derivative of the indefinite dyad in its simplest form. It is not indefinite plurality in general but an indefinite plurality of points or positions.

Plato's derivation of the soul from numbers may be seen in *Tim.* 35 b–36 b, where he represents the soul of the world as constituted by a grand musical scale. For the details of the derivation and for its significance we may refer to Professor Taylor's convincing account in his *Timaeus*, 136–146.

χρόνον δ' ἅμα καὶ οὐρανὸν καὶ ἕτερα δὴ πλείω. Usener thinks 6^b 3–4 T.'s meaning is that Plato omitted to give any account of the generation of time and of the heavens, as well as of many other things. He thinks that χρόνον, οὐρανόν, and ἕτερα πλείω are governed by παραλείπουσιν in ^a 27, and cannot stand in their present position. But neither can they be inserted in ^a 27, unless we read θ' ἅμα for δ' ἅμα. He holds, therefore, that this clause was a marginal note, or perhaps part of an alternative version, and must be removed from the text. He misses, however, the point of ἅμα, which links this clause up with what immediately precedes. For we can hardly be mistaken in connecting this passage with Arist. *Met.* 1072^a 2, where Aristotle says of Plato ὕστερον γάρ, καὶ ἅμα τῷ οὐρανῷ, ἡ ψυχή, ὥς φησίν. Aristotle infers from the late point at which the formation of the soul appears in the *Timaeus* (34 b) that Plato makes soul coeval with the heavens, and therefore later than the original disordered movement of *Tim.* 30 a.

56 COMMENTARY

6ᵇ 3-4 Again, *Tim.* 37 d–38 b would justify T. in saying that Plato generated time and the heavens simultaneously. We may assume, therefore, that ἅμα has its strict sense, and does not mean, as Usener takes it to mean, just 'also'. And in view of the rapidity and carelessness of T.'s style in this work there is no difficulty in supplying γεννῶσι in this clause from γεννήσαντες, ᵃ 25. For a similar *constructio ad sensum* cf. 5ᵃ 27 n.

4 τοῦ δ' οὐρανοῦ πέρι καὶ τῶν λοιπῶν οὐδεμίαν ἔτι ποιοῦνται μνείαν, i. e., though Plato describes the generation of the heaven, he does not go on to explain from his first principles the observed facts about its movement or those of the various celestial spheres, nor the concrete nature of the soul and of the other things he has derived from his first principles.

5 ὡσαύτως δ' οἱ περὶ Σπεύσιππον. This is an echo of Aristotle's complaint that Speusippus did not exhibit a continuous evolution of the universe from its first principles, but set up a large variety of types of entity and extemporized fresh principles to explain each type of entity; thus making the universe 'episodic, like a bad tragedy'. The only passage in which Aristotle charges Speusippus by name with this procedure is *Met.* 1028ᵇ 21–4, but with this we may certainly connect 1075ᵇ 37–1076ᵃ 3, 1090ᵇ 13–20. The charge that Speusippus did not attempt to give any coherent account of the genesis of the material world is borne out by the complete absence of physical treatises in Diogenes Laertius' list of his works (iv. 4 f.).

6-9 οὐδὲ ... θεῖα. The passage should be connected with Arist. *Met.* 1028ᵇ 24–7 ἔνιοι δὲ τὰ μὲν εἴδη καὶ τοὺς ἀριθμοὺς τὴν αὐτὴν ἔχειν φασὶ φύσιν, τὰ δὲ ἄλλα ἐχόμενα, γραμμὰς καὶ ἐπίπεδα, μέχρι πρὸς τὴν τοῦ οὐρανοῦ οὐσίαν καὶ τὰ αἰσθητά, and with Sext. Emp. *Adv. Math.* vii. 147, where Xenocrates is said to have recognized three kinds of substance: τὴν αἰσθητὴν οὐσίαν (τὴν ἐντὸς οὐρανοῦ), τὴν νοητήν (πάντων τῶν ἐκτὸς οὐρανοῦ), τὴν σύνθετον καὶ δοξαστήν (τὴν αὐτοῦ τοῦ οὐρανοῦ). The οὐρανός is described as composite because it is intelligible by means of astronomy and also perceptible by sight. Zeller (ii. 1.⁴ 1012, n. 7) thinks that T.'s μαθηματικά answers to Sextus Empiricus' third οὐσία, τὰ θεῖα forming no separate class but 'being found in the three others, so far as they are treated from a theological point of view'. But this is evidently a modern and unhistorical way of treating Xeno-

crates' doctrine. Further, we may take it as definitely implied 6ᵇ 6–9
by Aristotle's statements that Xenocrates identified the mathematical numbers with Ideas (cf. Ross, *Arist. Met.* I. lxxiv–lxxvi).
We must therefore suppose that νοητά and μαθηματικά in the present passage go closely together and do not stand for two of his three main classes of entity. And we are told further that he 'attributed a divine nature to the heavens, and called the stars fiery Olympian Gods' (Stob. *Anth.* i. p. 36. 12 W.). Taking the three main passages together, in the light of the further knowledge we have of Xenocrates' views, we seem to get the following hierarchy:

Aristotle.	Theophrastus.	Sextus Empiricus.
{τὰ εἴδη (= οἱ ἀριθμοί) = νοητά {γραμμαὶ καὶ ἐπίπεδα = μαθηματικά}		= ἡ νοητὴ οὐσία (πάντων τῶν ἐκτὸς οὐρανοῦ)
ἡ τοῦ οὐρανοῦ φύσις	= τὰ θεῖα	= ἡ σύνθετος καὶ δοξαστή (ἡ αὐτοῦ τοῦ οὐρανοῦ)
τὰ αἰσθητά	= αἰσθητά	= ἡ αἰσθητή (ἡ ἐντὸς οὐρανοῦ).

One point remains difficult. Why is intelligible substance described as that of the things outside the heavens? Whether the description is due to Xenocrates or is Sextus Empiricus' gloss, it is a loose phrase for the world of Ideas and mathematical objects. Everything else having been divided into the heavens and what is within the heavens (the terrestrial world), what remains is loosely described as outside the heavens, the truth being rather that it has no local habitation at all.

περιτίθησιν. It is doubtful whether περιτίθημι can have the 7 sense required, 'arranges' (its proper sense is seen in 7ᵃ 20 τὸ τοὺς λόγους ἑκάστοις περιθεῖναι); and Usener's conjecture διατίθησιν may well be right. περιτίθησιν would then be due to a copyist's eye having travelled forward to περὶ τὸν κόσμον.

πειρᾶται δὲ καὶ Ἑστιαῖος μέχρι τινός. Hestiaeus of Perinthus 9 (to be distinguished from the Pythagorean Hestiaeus of Tarentum) was a Platonist (*Ind. Hercul.* col. vi. 3, p. 34 Mekler; Diog. Laert. iii. 46) who edited the Platonic discourses on the Good (Simpl. *in Phys.* 453. 29). Opinions of his are recorded by Stobaeus (*Anth.* i. pp. 103. 2, 485. 7 W. = Diels, *Dox.* 318. 15, 403. 19).

εἰς τὰς ἰδέας ἀνάπτων, perhaps a reminiscence of Arist. *Met.* 13 1078ᵇ 22 τοὺς λόγους εἰς τοὺς ἀριθμοὺς ἀνῆπτον.

COMMENTARY

6ᵇ 13 ταύτας δ' εἰς τοὺς ἀριθμούς. This, if taken strictly, would mean that the numbers occupied, for Plato, a higher grade in the hierarchy of being than the Ideas. The numbers referred to cannot, of course, be the mathematical numbers, which were 'intermediate' between Ideas and sensible things. They must be the ideal numbers, i.e. the essences of the integers; and these are themselves Ideas. Thus the theory would be that the Idea-numbers form a superior class from which all other Ideas are derived. Against this we have to set Aristotle's repeated statement that in the Platonic theory the Ideas (i.e. all the Ideas) were numbers; cf. *Met.* 991ᵇ 9 εἴπερ εἰσὶν ἀριθμοὶ τὰ εἴδη, 992ᵇ 15 ταῦτα γὰρ οὔτε εἴδη οἷόν τε εἶναι (οὐ γάρ εἰσιν ἀριθμοί), 1073ᵃ 18 ἀριθμοὺς γὰρ λέγουσι τὰς ἰδέας οἱ λέγοντες ἰδέας, 1083ᵃ 17 εἴπερ εἰσὶν ἀριθμοὶ αἱ ἰδέαι, 1084ᵃ 7 εἰ πᾶσα ἰδέα τινὸς οἱ δὲ ἀριθμοὶ ἰδέαι (cf. 1081ᵃ 7). The present passage is the main evidence for M. Robin's view (*Théorie Platonicienne*, 454-61) that the Numbers were superior to the Ideas, and related to them as mathematical numbers were to sensible things. But we can hardly accept T.'s testimony against that of Aristotle, from whom he probably derived his knowledge of Plato's ἄγραφα δόγματα. T.'s testimony cannot be ignored, however, and it seems possible to reconcile his statement with those of Aristotle. Plato may be supposed to have reached his view in some such way as this: Reflecting on the nature of the straight line, he would observe that it is completely defined by two points in space, in the sense that through two given points one and only one straight line can pass. He therefore described 2 as the Form of the straight line. Similarly 3 was the Form of the plane. And since the simplest rectilinear solid, the tetrahedron, is completely determined if we can give its four corner-points, 4 was the Form of the solid. From this he seems to have reached the general view that for each entity there is some number which states its structure and nature in the most abstract possible way; thus each Form was said to be a number. But the same number might be the Form of more than one thing. E.g., 4 was the Form of justice as well as of the solid, since justice involves two persons, and two 'honours or possessions' to be divided between them. The solid and justice could therefore be regarded as the number 4 manifested in two different materials, and a higher point of

COMMENTARY

abstraction was reached when one spoke of 'the number 4' than 6ᵇ 13 when one spoke of 'the Form of the solid' or of 'the Form of justice'. Thus Aristotle is justified in characterizing the theory by saying that the Platonists described the Forms as numbers, rather than by saying that they described the numbers as Forms; and T. is justified in saying that they linked the Forms up with the numbers as with something superior to them. Cf. Ross, *Arist. Met.* I. lxvii–lxix.

τὰς ἀρχάς, i.e. the One and the indefinite dyad. 14

τῶν εἰρημένων, i.e. such things as τόπος, κενόν, ἄπειρον, ψυχή, 15 χρόνος, οὐρανός (ll. 1–3).

ἔνιοι δὲ καὶ τὴν ἀλήθειαν ἐν τούτοις. For the ellipse cf. 5ᵃ 27 n. 16 τούτοις = ταῖς ἀρχαῖς (cf. 5ᵃ 25 n.).

ἐκείνοις = ταῖς ἄλλαις μεθόδοις (cf. 5ᵃ 25 n.). 19

τὰ μετὰ τὰς ἀρχὰς ἰσχυρότερα καὶ οἷον τελεώτερα τῶν ἐπιστημῶν. τῶν ἐπιστημῶν is a partitive genitive depending on τὰ μετὰ τὰς ἀρχάς. The contrast seems to be between metaphysics and the mathematical sciences. In the latter, the further we get from the ἀρχαί—i.e. as we advance from the point to the line, the plane, and the solid—the 'stronger' and 'more complete' (i.e. more concrete; cf. ὡς ἐν ἀμφοῖν τὸ τέλεον ὄν, 7ᵃ 8) are the entities we arrive at; whereas the metaphysics of the Platonists treats the simplest ἀρχαί, i.e. the One and the indefinite dyad, and after them the numbers, as the truest reality. This difference, T. adds (ll. 20–2), is natural enough; in the mathematical sciences the main interest is in deduction from the ἀρχαί, in metaphysics it is in the establishment of the ἀρχαί; and it is natural that people should describe as the truest reality that in which they are most interested.

ἔνθα μὲν γὰρ τῶν ἀρχῶν, ἐν δὲ ταῖς λοιπαῖς ἀπὸ τῶν ἀρχῶν ἡ 21 ζήτησις, a reminiscence of Arist. *E. N.* 1095ᵃ 32 εὖ γὰρ καὶ ὁ Πλάτων ἠπόρει τοῦτο καὶ ἐζήτει πότερον ἀπὸ τῶν ἀρχῶν ἢ ἐπὶ τὰς ἀρχάς ἐστιν ἡ ὁδός, and of the contrast between metaphysics (νόησις) and science (διάνοια) in the Divided Line, *Rep.* 511 a b, where science is described as οὐκ ἐπ' ἀρχὴν ἰοῦσαν, ὡς οὐ δυναμένην τῶν ὑποθέσεων ἀνωτέρω ἐκβαίνειν, while the philosopher proceeds τὰς ὑποθέσεις ποιούμενος οὐκ ἀρχὰς ἀλλὰ τῷ ὄντι ὑποθέσεις, οἷον ἐπιβάσεις τε καὶ ὁρμάς, ἵνα μέχρι τοῦ ἀνυποθέτου ἐπὶ τὴν τοῦ παντὸς ἀρχὴν ἰών, ... οὕτως ἐπὶ τελευτὴν καταβαίνῃ.

COMMENTARY

6ᵇ 25 ὅσοι πῦρ, i. e. Heraclitus and Hippasus; cf. Heraclitus, fr. 30, 90, Arist. *Met.* 984ᵃ 7, Theophr. *Phys. Opin.* fr. 1 (Diels, *Dox.* 475. 14).

καὶ γῆν. Aristotle says that none of the natural philosophers treated earth as a first principle, but points out that popular thought and the poets (e. g. Hesiod) did so (*Met.* 989ᵃ 8-12). Later writers described Xenophanes as having treated earth as the primary element (Diels, *Vors.*³ i. 52. 28), but T. in his Φυσικῶν Δόξαι did not do so (ib. 53. 1–3).

ὅσοι πῦρ καὶ γῆν *may*, however, be a reference to the presumably Pythagorean cosmology described in Parmenides' Way of Opinion (cf. Arist. *Met.* 986ᵇ 34, *Phys.* 186ᵃ 20-22, *De Gen. et Corr.* 318ᵇ 6, 330ᵇ 14; Theophr. *Phys. Opin.* fr. 6, 6ᵃ in Diels, *Dox.*; Hippol. i. 11). But the elements named in the Way of Opinion are actually fire and night (i.e. mist, air, or void) (fr. 8. 56-9). Later in the history of Pythagoreanism, fire and earth probably came to be treated as the primary elements (cf. Pl. *Tim.* 31 b and Burnet, *E. G. P.* § 147), and this may account for Aristotle's and Theophrastus' reading that view into the Way of Opinion. Cf. Ross, *Arist. Met.* 984ᵇ 4.

The general reference is to the early thinkers who described the material universe as formed by differentiation out of a comparatively indefinite material in which it was potentially present.

27 ἐν τῷ Τιμαίῳ, 30 a βουληθεὶς γὰρ ὁ θεὸς ἀγαθὰ μὲν πάντα, φλαῦρον δὲ μηδὲν εἶναι κατὰ δύναμιν, οὕτω δὴ πᾶν ὅσον ἦν ὁρατὸν παραλαβὼν οὐχ ἡσυχίαν ἄγον ἀλλὰ κινούμενον πλημμελῶς καὶ ἀτάκτως, εἰς τάξιν αὐτὸ ἤγαγεν ἐκ τῆς ἀταξίας, ἡγησάμενος ἐκεῖνο τούτου πάντως ἄμεινον.

7ᵃ 2 καθά περ ἐν γραμματικῇ καὶ μουσικῇ καὶ ταῖς μαθηματικαῖς, i. e. all these sciences treat their subject-matter not as proceeding by differentiation from an inchoate mass, but as built up out of perfectly definite elements—the letters, the primary intervals, points, lines, and planes.

3 συνακολουθεῖ. Usener's συνακολουθεῖν would be more elegant, but it does not seem necessary to depart from the manuscript reading.

5 καὶ τὰ ὄργανα καὶ τὰ ἄλλα κατὰ τὰς ἀρχάς. I. e., the ἀρχαί in the arts are perfectly definite, and upon them depend the instruments and the processes used. T. means that, for instance, the

COMMENTARY 61

drugs used by the medical art are determined by the nature of 7ª 5
health, which is the ἀρχή of the art.

οἱ μὲν ἐμμόρφους πάσας probably refers to the Pythagoreans and 6-7
Platonists, οἱ δὲ μόνον τὰς ὑλικάς to the bulk of the pre-Socratic
schools, οἱ δ' ἄμφω to Aristotle.

κἀκείνοις, i. e. even to those who emphasize the material prin- 10
ciples alone (l. 7).

ἐν τάξει καὶ λόγῳ καὶ μορφαῖς καὶ δυνάμεσιν καὶ περιόδοις. μορφαῖς, 12
&c., may be treated either as co-ordinate with τάξει and λόγῳ, or
as datives of 'respect' depending on these words. In view of
10ᵇ 22 f. the latter interpretation (first adopted by Usener) is
perhaps the more probable.

"ὥσπερ σάρμα εἰκῇ κεχυμένων ὁ κάλλιστος", φησὶν Ἡράκλειτος, 14
"[ὁ] κόσμος". Earlier editors treat ὁ κάλλιστος κόσμος alone as
a quotation from Heraclitus, but Diels is doubtless right in
recognizing a longer quotation (fr. 124). Either his σάρμα or
Bernays's σάρον (in the same sense) is pretty certainly the correct
emendation of the manuscript reading σάρξ, which is meaningless
in the context. σάρμα was used by the third-century comic poet
Rhinthon (fr. 25 Kaibel); σάρον was used by Sophron in the fifth
century (fr. 160 Kaibel), by Ion of Chios (fr. 9 Nauck), and by
Callimachus (Del. 225). It is not necessary to emend κεχυμένων.
στράγξ and σωρός are less likely emendations of σάρξ. στράγξ
gives an unsuitable sense, and though σωρός gives a good sense
and derives some support from Arist. Met. 1040ᵇ 9, 1041ᵇ 12,
1045ᵃ 9, it is hard to see why so common a word should have
been corrupted. For the thought Diels aptly compares Heraclitus fr. 52 αἰὼν παῖς ἐστι παίζων, πεττεύων· παιδὸς ἡ βασιληίη.

"ὁ κάλλιστος", φησὶν Ἡράκλειτος, "[ὁ] κόσμος". The order of
the words is chosen in order to emphasize κάλλιστος and
bring out the contrast with σάρμα εἰκῇ κεχυμένων. The second
ὁ is no doubt due to a copyist who took ὁ κάλλιστος with
Ἡράκλειτος.

καὶ . . . εἶναι. Usener brackets these words, as being part of 15-19
a fuller alternative version of the previous sentence. Really this
sentence is a proper part of the argument. Even the advocates
of material causes alone would have to admit that it would be
strange if the world were orderly and its ἀρχαί not so (ll. 10-15).
But they assume orderliness, even in the minutest detail, with

62   COMMENTARY

7ᵃ 15–19 regard to lifeless and living things alike, and yet assume the ἀρχαί to be indefinite (ll. 15–19).

18 καί περ αὐτομάτως γινομένων. The reference is to the spontaneous generation from mud, &c., which the ancients believed to take place in the case of many of the lower animals—fishes (Arist. *H. A.* 569ᵃ 11), testaceans (ib. 547ᵇ 18, *G. Ä.* 761ᵇ 23), insects (*H. A.* 539ᵃ 24, *G. A.* 732ᵇ 12).

19–ᵇ 5 Χαλεπὸν ... ἡλίου. T. now turns from criticizing the maintainers of indeterminate ἀρχαί (ll. 10–19) to point out the difficulties in maintaining determinate ἀρχαί.

23 τῇ ἑτέρων τάξει. ἀστέρων is a plausible but unnecessary emendation of ἑτέρων. The point here is simply that many things in nature cannot be explained by reference to a final cause of their own, but are effects of order and change in something else. The 'something else' T. actually has in mind is the celestial system, but this is not mentioned till ᵇ 5.

7ᵇ 3 τὰς ὥρας τὰς ἐτησίους. ἐτήσιος does not seem to be found in the sense of 'of the trade-winds' (οἱ ἐτησίαι), i. e. 'of summer'. It means simply 'annual'.

7 μέχρι πόσου, i. e. how far down in the universe. T.'s own view is intermediate between the two extreme views about τάξις discussed in ᵃ 10–19, 19–ᵇ 5.

8 τὸ πλέον, i. e. more order.

ἢ εἰς τὸ χεῖρον ἡ μετάβασις is explained by 11ᵇ 7–12. The suggestion is that the universe needs the co-operation of opposite principles, so that if it is to be maintained at all, there must be some unorderliness in it as well as some order.

10 τὸ περὶ τῆς ἠρεμίας, i. e. the view that the first principles are static and unchanging, which is common ground to Plato and Aristotle (cf. 4ᵃ 5–8).

13 The stop after ἀνάψει must be a comma, not as in most editions a full stop, since what follows is one form of the view that regards ἠρεμία as a mere negation.

ἀντιμεταλλακτέον. The word is unknown elsewhere, and Usener substitutes ἀντικαταλλακτέον. But there is no objection to ἀντιμεταλλακτέον, in which both ἀντί and μετά preserve their meaning. 'Instead of "rest", "activity" must be substituted for "movement".' For the form cf. ἀντιμεταβαίνω, -βάλλω, -κλίνω, &c.

15 ἐν τοῖς αἰσθητοῖς. Usener brackets ἐν on the ground that the

COMMENTARY 63

verb to be supplied is ἀναπτέον. But in this loose kind of style 7ᵇ 15 there is no difficulty in supplying something like θετέον εἶναι.

ἐπεὶ τό γε διὰ τοῦτ' ἠρεμεῖν ὡς ἀδύνατον ἀεὶ κινούμενον εἶναι τὸ κινοῦν—οὐ γὰρ ἂν εἴη πρῶτον—κίνδυνος μὴ λογῶδες. Written as Usener writes it, with a dash before οὐ and none after πρῶτον, the sentence is a complete anacoluthon, and this is cured by treating οὐ . . . πρῶτον as parenthetical. But the manuscript reading ὡς ἀδύνατον ἀεὶ κινοῦν εἶναι τὸ κινοῦν—οὐ γὰρ ἂν εἴη πρῶτον remains unintelligible. It makes no sense to say, 'that which imparts movement cannot be always imparting it—for then it would not be the first thing'. Nor does Usener's emendation of the second κινοῦν to κινούμενον mend matters. There is no sense in 'that which is in movement cannot be always imparting movement—for then it would not be the first thing'. What is needed is to change the *first* κινοῦν to κινούμενον. We then get the intelligible remark: 'Since the view that the first principle must be at rest for this reason, that that which imparts movement cannot at each stage be itself in movement—for then it would not be the first thing—is suspiciously like a merely verbal argument.' The argument so described is: 'Y may move Z through being itself moved by X, and X may move Y through being itself moved by W, and other terms in the series YXW . . . may cause movement in this way, but this cannot be so at every stage; for a thing which imparts movement by being itself moved is obviously not the first thing but implies a prior thing to move it.' This is the argument of Aristotle in *Met.* 1072ᵃ 24 f. ἐπεὶ δὲ τὸ κινούμενον καὶ κινοῦν [καὶ] μέσον, †τοίνυν† ἐστί τι ὃ οὐ κινούμενον κινεῖ. As against Aristotle's view that there must be an unmoved first mover, T. wants to suggest that the first mover may be a self-mover (cf. ll. 19–22).

λογῶδες. The meaning 'prosaic' (which occurs in Aristox. 18 *Harm.* p. 18 Meibom) does not seem very suitable here, and probably the word means 'verbal', like λογικός in Aristotle.

μείζω τινὰ αἰτίαν ζητεῖ, cf. 5ᵃ 22.

δοκεῖ . . . πάσχειν. T. appeals to the apparent facts of the 19–22 initiation of self-movement by men and animals.

κινεῖ, the manuscript reading, is perfectly right if taken as 21 governing ὅ.

διὰ τὸ ποιεῖν καὶ πάσχειν may be retained, in the sense of

7ᵇ 21 'because of the distinction of action and passivity', i. e. because the one is agent and the other is patient. But it is very tempting to read διὰ τὸ ⟨τὸ⟩ ποιοῦν καὶ πάσχειν, 'because that which acts is also acted on'; cf. Arist. *G. A.* 768ᵇ 16 τὸ ποιοῦν καὶ πάσχει ὑπὸ τοῦ πάσχοντος.

22-3 ἔτι ... θεόν. The point seems to be that in God there is a self-realizing activity which transcends the distinction between mover and moved.

23 ἄτοπον δὲ καὶ τὸ ἕτερον λεχθέν, ὡς οὐ μιμοῦνται τὰ ὀρεγόμενα τοῦ ἠρεμοῦντος, 'strange too is the other thing that has been maintained, that the things that desire what is at rest do not imitate it', sc. by being at rest themselves. This is the same criticism that has been made in 5ᵃ 23-7 ἄπορον δὲ καὶ πῶς ποτε φυσικὴν ὄρεξιν ἐχόντων οὐ τὴν ἠρεμίαν διώκουσιν ἀλλὰ τὴν κίνησιν. τί οὖν ἅμα τῇ μιμήσει φασὶν ἐκεῖνο ὁμοίως ὅσοι τε τὸ ἓν καὶ ὅσοι τοὺς ἀριθμοὺς λέγουσιν; The emendation κινοῦνται for μιμοῦνται is unnecessary and misleading.

8ᵃ 2 τί γὰρ αὐτοῖς οὐ συνακολουθεῖ ἡ τῶν ἄλλων; sc. ἠρεμία, to be understood from ἠρεμοῦντος, l. 1. For the *constructio ad sensum* cf. 5ᵃ 27 n. This reading is somewhat nearer to that of the manuscripts, and gives a better sense than that of Usener. For συνακολουθεῖ cf. 7ᵃ 3.

3-7 πλὴν ... τελεώτατον. T. here answers the objection raised by himself in 7ᵇ 23-8ᵃ 2 very much as in 6ᵃ 2-5 he answers the objection raised by himself in 5ᵇ 26-6ᵃ 2. In both cases the answer is that the kind of unity we should expect to find is not that of an indivisible whole but that of a system.

12 ᾗ δὲ γένεσις, ἡ οὐσία γ' αὐτῶν τῷ μορφοῦσθαι κατὰ τοὺς λόγους. These words should be connected closely with, and not as in most editions separated by a full stop from, what precedes. They belong to the statement of the second alternative, according to which matter is not unreal (as in ll. 10 f.) but is real though indefinite (ll. 11 f.); for it is this alternative from which a conclusion is drawn in what follows (ll. 14-19). But the ellipse of ἔστι with ᾗ δὲ γένεσις is rather difficult, and possibly we should read ἀόριστον δὲ καθά περ ἐν ταῖς τέχναις ἡ γένεσις (sc. ἐξ ἀορίστου ἐστίν), ἡ οὐσία δ' κτλ.; or read ἡ δὲ γένεσις ἢ οὐσία γ' ('the becoming or rather the being') for ᾗ δὲ γένεσις, ἡ οὐσία γ'.

19 κατ' ἀναλογίαν ληπτέον ἐπὶ τὰς τέχνας. We are unable to quote

COMMENTARY

a parallel for the use of ἐπί with κατ' ἀναλογίαν, but it seems quite 8ᵃ 19 possible that ἐπί should be so used, and if so, a rather better sense is got by retaining it and taking ληπτέον as = 'matter is to be understood' (cf. λαμβάνειν 4ᵇ 14) than by reading ἐστί and taking τὰς τέχνας as the object of ληπτέον.

For the thought cf. Arist. *Phys.* 191ᵃ 7–12 ἡ δ' ὑποκειμένη φύσις ἐπιστητὴ κατ' ἀναλογίαν. ὡς γὰρ πρὸς ἀνδριάντα χαλκὸς ἢ πρὸς κλίνην ξύλον ἢ πρὸς τῶν ἄλλων τι τῶν ἐχόντων μορφὴν [ἢ ὕλη καὶ] τὸ ἄμορφον ἔχει πρὶν λαβεῖν τὴν μορφήν, οὕτως αὕτη πρὸς οὐσίαν ἔχει καὶ τὸ τόδε τι καὶ τὸ ὄν.

τί δή ποτε ἡ φύσις καὶ ἡ ὅλη δ' οὐσία τοῦ παντὸς ἐν ἐναντίοις ἐστίν, 22 καὶ σχεδὸν ἰσομοιρεῖ τὸ χεῖρον τῷ βελτίονι. The doctrine of the good and evil principles as co-ordinate elements of the universe is found in the Pythagoreans. It is opposed by Aristotle; cf. *Met.* 1051ᵃ 17 οὐκ ἔστι τὸ κακὸν παρὰ τὰ πράγματα, 1075ᵇ 21 οὐ γάρ ἐστιν ἐναντίον τῷ πρώτῳ οὐδέν.

ἐν ἐναντίοις ἐστίν, 'is contained in contraries' or 'depends on 23 contraries' (ἐν being used as in such phrases as ἕξις ἐν μεσότητι οὖσα Arist. *E. N.* 1106ᵇ 36; εἰσὶ αἱ εἰρημέναι φιλίαι ἐν ἰσότητι ib. 1158ᵇ 1).

Εὐριπίδην, in the *Aeolus*, fr. 21. 3 Nauck. 26

For the thought of the sentence cf. 6ᵃ 2–5. 27-ᵇ 4

οὐθὲν . . . αὐτοῖς. I. e., there are not merely ἐναντία ἐν τῷ αὐτῷ 8ᵇ 2–4 γένει (like white and black) but also ἐναντία γένη. Cf. Theophr. fr. 15 ἐπεὶ δὲ ἐναντίαι τῶν ἐναντίων αἱ ἀρχαί, δῆλον ὅτι οὐδ' ἐν ἑνὶ γένει ταῦτα, καθάπερ οὐδὲ τὸ ἀγαθὸν καὶ κακόν, καὶ κίνησις καὶ στάσις.

The *further* paradox referred to is contained in οὐχ οἷόν τε. It 4 f. is more paradoxical to say that being necessarily involves contraries than to say that in fact it is contained in or depends on them.

The view referred to appears to be the Atomists' doctrine of 6–8 the void. Cf. Theophr. *Phys. Opin.* fr. 8 (in Diels, *Dox.* 483. 19–484. 1) ἔτι δὲ οὐδὲν μᾶλλον τὸ ὂν ἢ τὸ μὴ ὂν ὑπάρχειν, καὶ αἴτια ὁμοίως εἶναι τοῖς γινομένοις ἄμφω. τὴν γὰρ τῶν ἀτόμων οὐσίαν ναστὴν καὶ πλήρη ὑποτιθέμενος ὂν ἔλεγεν εἶναι καὶ ἐν τῷ κενῷ φέρεσθαι, ὅπερ μὴ ὂν ἐκάλει καὶ οὐκ ἔλαττον τοῦ ὄντος εἶναί φησι.

ὑπερβατός τις σοφία, cf. 6ᵃ 3. 9

εἴ τε γὰρ ἕτερα ἀλλήλων . . . ἔν τε τοῖς καθόλου . . . There is no 17 f. clearly thought out distinction between the two cases suggested

8ᵇ 17 f. **by τε... τε.** εἴ τε γὰρ ἕτερα ἀλλήλων is quite general, applying alike to the cases of generic difference, specific difference, and numerical difference; in ἔν τε τοῖς καθόλου κτλ. the latter two cases are dealt with separately.

18 The comma usually printed after ὄντων must be removed (as by Wimmer); πλειόνων ὄντων τῶν ὑπὸ τὰ καθόλου goes together.

23 ἦν ἄν, an instance of the iterative use of ἄν (L. and S., new ed., s.v. ἄν (C)), = 'would be found to have been'.

24-7 **ὅλως ... ἀμφοῖν.** This sentence seems to stand in opposition to what has gone before. 'Though science studies peculiar properties, i. e. properties not absolutely general but confined to determinate subjects, yet it is always grasping an identity in difference.' I. e., it never studies the individual, but the specific, that which, while not true of all subjects, is true of more than one. Usener's reading ὁμοίως is incompatible with this opposition; the manuscript reading ὅλως is compatible with it; but ὅμως would be even more suitable, and has therefore some probability.

25 **ἤτοι κοινῇ καὶ καθόλου λεγόμενον ἢ ἰδίᾳ πως καθ' ἕκαστον.** The universal, T. intimates, may either be predicable without difference of the various things of which it is predicable, or with a difference in each case, as quantitativeness, equality, and the like are predicable with a difference of numbers and of lines, meaning in the one case discrete quantitativeness or numerical equality, and in the other continuous quantitativeness or equality in length; and as life, nutrition, &c., can be predicated of animals and plants only with a difference. κοινῇ καὶ καθόλου λεγόμενον seems to refer to specific and ἰδίᾳ πως καθ' ἕκαστον to generic identity.

9ᵃ 1 ἐνίων μὲν καθόλου seems to be a necessary correction of the manuscript reading ἔνια τῶν μὲν καθόλου. 'In some cases there is a universal end', i. e. the end is a universal. Wimmer's ἐνίων μὲν τὸ καθόλου gives a better opposition to τῶν δὲ τὸ ἐν μέρει, but we should hardly be justified in inserting the τό. Usener's ἔνθα τῶν μὲν καθόλου gives no good sense.

The opposition is between science on the one hand and conduct and art on the other.

4 **οὕτως γὰρ αὐτῶν ἡ ἐνέργεια.** Things to be done and things to be made exist only as individual acts and individual objects.

4, 7 **Ταὐτῷ, τό.** In l. 4 P reads ταυτωι, the other manuscripts ταὐτό,

in 7 all read τό. Usener reads ταὐτῷ and τῷ. It would be pre- 9ᵃ 4, 7
ferable to read ταὐτό and τό, assuming ταὐτό to have been
corrupted to ταυτωι in P because it was thought to be co-ordinated
by καί with οὐσίᾳ, &c. But it is still better to follow the best
manuscript reading and take the construction to be different in
the two clauses, as we have done in our translation.

διαιρέσεις. A nominative seems to be required after εἰ ἄρα. 6
Cf. 8ᵃ 19 κατ' ἀναλογίαν . . . καὶ εἴ τις ὁμοιότης ἄλλη.

ἀπέχοντος. It seems impossible to make sense of ἀπέχοντες, 7
which has probably been introduced through the influence of
δι' ἡμᾶς αὐτούς.

τὰ μὲν . . . τὰ δὲ . . . τὰ δέ are adverbial, as they often are from 8–9
Herodotus onwards.

τὰ ἐν ἀρχῇ καὶ τὰ ἑπόμενα μέχρι ζῴων καὶ φυτῶν καὶ ἐσχάτων τῶν 13
ἀψύχων. The order is peculiar; one would expect the order to
be—'elements, comparatively simple (inorganic) compounds,
higher compounds (i.e. plants and animals)'. The order in-
tended is, however, neither one of increasing complication nor
one of temporal succession but presumably one of dignity. Presumably then τὰ ἐν ἀρχῇ refers to the heavenly bodies.

ὥσπερ καὶ ἐν τοῖς μαθηματικοῖς, i.e. just as mathematics recog- 16
nizes different properties as belonging respectively to numbers,
lines, planes, and solids.

ἔχει . . . ἱκανῶς. Usener remarks that this sentence is super- 16-18
fluous in view of the preceding ὥσπερ ἐν τοῖς μαθηματικοῖς, and
should perhaps be considered an alternative version of it. This
does not seem probable. The sentence adds a new point. Not
only have the various kinds of mathematical objects (μαθηματικά)
their distinctive attributes, but the mathematical studies themselves (μαθήματα) have correspondingly different characters. Cf.
Arist. Met. 1004ᵃ 2–9, 1026ᵃ 25–7.

διῄρηται δ' ἱκανῶς can hardly refer to 8ᵇ 26, which is the briefest 18
possible allusion to the subject. The reference is more general—
'the distinction has been sufficiently well threshed out in the
School'.

εἰ δὲ καὶ ἔνια γνωστὰ τῷ ἄγνωστα εἶναι, καθά περ τινές φασιν. The
reference is to a dialectical argument quoted in Arist. Rhet.
1402ᵃ 4–7, presumably from some sophist: ἐν μὲν τοῖς διαλεκτικοῖς
(sc. γίγνεται φαινόμενος συλλογισμός) . . . ὅτι ἐπιστητὸν τὸ ἄγνωστον,

9ᵃ 18 ἔστιν γὰρ ἐπιστητὸν τὸ ἄγνωστον ὅτι ἄγνωστον, 'the unknown is known, for it is known to be unknown'.

21-3 τάχα ... ἀόρατον. T. rejects the sophistic argument given in our last note, and insists that the unknown, if it is to come to be known, must come to be known by virtue of some analogy with the known; it is a mere play on words to say it can be known because it can be known to be unknown. This would be like saying that the unseen can be seen because it can be seen to be unseen. The argument therefore requires us to read τῷ ἀοράτῳ τὸ ἀόρατον in l. 23, with the editors earlier than Brandis.

9ᵇ 1 ᾗ κτλ. The manuscripts have η. At one time Usener suggested (with no great probability) ἔστι δέ. In his edition he takes the view that there is a hiatus here in which stood a definition of science as being knowledge of causes, and suggests that η may be a relic of something like ἡγούμεθ' οὖν ἐπίστασθαι ... We have argued in the Introduction (p. xxi) against the supposition of a hiatus. ἢ καί should, we think, be written ᾗ καί, which is a favourite opening in this work. Cf. 10ᵇ 26 ᾗ καὶ ἔοικεν ὁ λόγος ἔχειν τι πιστόν, 11ᵇ 7 ᾗ (our reading) καὶ τὰς ἀρχὰς ἐναντίας, and De Sensu 64 ᾗ καὶ φανερὸν ὡς κτλ. The connexion of the clause with what precedes is brought out in our Introduction, pp. xxi-xxii.

6 ἄμφω, i. e. τὰ αἰσθητά and τὰ νοητά.

ἡ μὲν ἡμῖν ἡ δ' ἁπλῶς, cf. Arist. An. Post. 71ᵇ 33 πρότερα δ' ἐστὶ καὶ γνωριμώτερα διχῶς· οὐ γὰρ ταὐτὸν πρότερον τῇ φύσει καὶ πρὸς ἡμᾶς πρότερον, οὐδὲ γνωριμώτερον καὶ ἡμῖν γνωριμώτερον. λέγω δὲ πρὸς ἡμᾶς μὲν πρότερα καὶ γνωριμώτερα τὰ ἐγγύτερον τῆς αἰσθήσεως, ἁπλῶς δὲ πρότερα καὶ γνωριμώτερα τὰ πορρώτερον. Phys. 184ᵃ 16 πέφυκε δὲ ἐκ τῶν γνωριμωτέρων ἡμῖν ἡ ὁδὸς καὶ σαφεστέρων ἐπὶ τὰ σαφέστερα τῇ φύσει καὶ γνωριμώτερα· οὐ γὰρ ταὐτὰ ἡμῖν τε γνώριμα καὶ ἁπλῶς.

8 δυνάμεθα δι' αἰτίου θεωρεῖν, ἀρχὰς ἀπὸ τῶν αἰσθήσεων λαμβάνοντες. The doctrine is that of An. Post. 88ᵃ 2-6, where, after pointing out that sense-perception is not scientific knowledge, Aristotle adds οὐ μὴν ἀλλ' ἐκ τοῦ θεωρεῖν τοῦτο πολλάκις συμβαῖνον τὸ καθόλου ἂν θηρεύσαντες ἀπόδειξιν εἴχομεν· ἐκ γὰρ τῶν καθ' ἕκαστα πλειόνων τὸ καθόλου δῆλον. τὸ δὲ καθόλου τίμιον, ὅτι δηλοῖ τὸ αἴτιον. The transition from sense-perception to science through memory and 'experience' is described more fully in An. Post. ii. 19 and Met. A. 1.

COMMENTARY

ὅταν δὲ ἐπ' αὐτὰ τὰ ἄκρα καὶ πρῶτα μεταβαίνωμεν, οὐκέτι δυνάμεθα, 9ᵇ 10 we can no longer give causal explanations. This seems to be a reminiscence of *An. Post.* 88ᵃ 6–8 ὥστε περὶ τῶν τοιούτων ἡ καθόλου τιμιωτέρα τῶν αἰσθήσεων καὶ τῆς νοήσεως, ὅσων ἕτερον τὸ αἴτιον· περὶ δὲ τῶν πρώτων ἄλλος λόγος.

εἴτε . . . βλέπειν. The passage is a reminiscence of Arist. *Met.* 11–13 993ᵇ 7–11 ἴσως δὲ καὶ τῆς χαλεπότητος οὔσης κατὰ δύο τρόπους, οὐκ ἐν τοῖς πράγμασιν ἀλλ' ἐν ἡμῖν τὸ αἴτιον αὐτῆς· ὥσπερ γὰρ τὰ τῶν νυκτερίδων ὄμματα πρὸς τὸ φέγγος ἔχει τὸ μεθ' ἡμέραν, οὕτω καὶ τῆς ἡμετέρας ψυχῆς ὁ νοῦς πρὸς τὰ τῇ φύσει φανερώτατα πάντων.

In l. 13 Usener's conjecture βλέποντες is attractive, but it seems possible to retain βλέπειν, either as depending on δυνάμεθα (with a comma after ἀσθένειαν) or preferably as depending on ἀσθένειαν. Cf. Dem. 23. 54 ἀσθενέστερος . . . ἐνεγκεῖν πόνον and *Il.* ii. 451 f. σθένος . . . πολεμίζειν, Aesch. *Eum.* 87 σθένος . . . ποιεῖν εὖ.

θιγόντι καὶ οἷον ἀψαμένῳ, διὸ καὶ οὐκ ἔστιν ἀπάτη περὶ αὐτά. Cf. 15 Arist. *Met.* 1051ᵇ 24–6 (about τὰ ἀσύνθετα) τὸ μὲν θιγεῖν καὶ φάναι ἀληθές (οὐ γὰρ ταὐτὸ κατάφασις καὶ φάσις), τὸ δ' ἀγνοεῖν μὴ θιγγάνειν (ἀπατηθῆναι γὰρ περὶ τὸ τί ἐστιν οὐκ ἔστιν ἀλλ' ἢ κατὰ συμβεβηκός), 1072ᵇ 20–21 νοητὸς γὰρ γίγνεται (*sc.* ὁ νοῦς) θιγγάνων καὶ νοῶν. There is no error possible (except incidentally) with regard to τὰ ἄκρα καὶ πρῶτα because our state of mind towards them is not one of affirmation but of simple apprehension, the opposite of which is not error but nescience. τὸ δὲ ψεῦδος οὐκ ἔστιν, οὐδὲ ἀπάτη, ἀλλ' ἄγνοια, *Met.* 1052ᵃ 1.

τὰς τῆς φύσεως connects with τὰς καθ' ἕκαστα πραγματείας l. 18, 20 and τὰς ἔτι προτέρας, i. e. metaphysical inquiries, with τὰς μεγίστας l. 19.

οἱ γὰρ ἁπάντων ζητοῦντες λόγον ἀναιροῦσιν λόγον. Cf. Arist. *Met.* 21 1011ᵃ 12 λόγον ζητοῦσιν ὧν οὐκ ἔστι λόγος· ἀποδείξεως γὰρ ἀρχὴ οὐκ ἀπόδειξίς ἐστιν, 1012ᵃ 20 οἱ μὲν οὖν διὰ τοιαύτην αἰτίαν λέγουσιν, οἱ δὲ διὰ τὸ πάντων ζητεῖν λόγον, 1063ᵇ 7–11 πρὸς μὲν οὖν τοὺς ἐκ λόγου τὰς εἰρημένας ἀπορίας ἔχοντας οὐ ῥᾴδιον διαλῦσαι μὴ τιθέντων τι καὶ τούτου μηκέτι λόγον ἀπαιτούντων· οὕτω γὰρ πᾶς λόγος καὶ πᾶσα ἀπόδειξις γίγνεται· μηθὲν γὰρ τιθέντες ἀναιροῦσι τὸ διαλέγεσθαι καὶ ὅλως λόγον. From Theophr. *Phys. Opin.* fr. 10 (Diels, *Dox.* 485. 6–16) it seems that it is against Plato that T. aims this criticism.

After πέφυκεν Usener marks a lacuna, but without sufficient 24

COMMENTARY

9ᵇ 24 reason; cf. Introduction, pp. xxii–xxiii. It seems enough to insert δέ after ὅσοι.

25 τὰ κατὰ τὰς φοράς, sc. ὑπολαμβάνουσιν.

25–7 τὰ μεγέθη, τὰ σχήματα, τὰς ἀποστάσεις seems to be co-ordinate with τὰς φοράς; ὅσα ἄλλα is apparently co-ordinate with τὰ κατὰ τὰς φοράς.

10ᵃ 1 τά τε πρῶτα κινοῦντα seems to refer partly to the πρῶτον κινοῦν ἀκίνητον, i. e. God, and partly to the πρῶτα κινοῦντα καὶ κινούμενα, i. e. the spheres of the stars.

4 καθ' ἕκαστον τῶν εἰδῶν ἢ μερῶν ἄχρι ζῴων καὶ φυτῶν. The objects of study coming between the heavenly bodies (ll. 1–3) and living things are presumably the things studied in Aristotle's *Meteorologica*, the layers of fire and air that come between the heavenly bodies and the earth's surface.

6 τοῖς πρώτοις ... τῆς φύσεως here must refer to the πρῶτον κινοῦν ἀκίνητον (cf. l. 1).

8 ὁ τρόπος. Usener, taking this to mean 'the method of astronomy', thinks there is a reference to the views of Epicurus, and compares Epic. *Epist.* ii. 113 τῶν τὴν ματαίαν ἀστρολογίαν ἐζηλωκότων καὶ εἰς τὸ κενὸν αἰτίας τινῶν ἀποδιδόντων. But there is no great resemblance between the two passages. In view of the preceding clauses, ll. 5–7, it seems more likely that ὁ τρόπος is 'the method of the study of τὰ κυριώτατα καὶ πρότερα' (i. e. of philosophy), and in this case the reference in ὡς οἴονταί τινες is probably to Aristotle's distinction between the method of metaphysics and that of natural philosophy. The phrase ὁ τρόπος οὐ φυσικός is a reminiscence of Arist. *Met.* 995ᵃ 16 οὐ φυσικὸς ὁ τρόπος, but the meaning there is different—that the mathematical method is not suitable to physics since physical things always contain matter.

9–10 καίτοι ... οὐρανοῦ. Though the study of the οὐρανός has partly to be conducted, as T. has been saying, by a philosophical method distinct from the physical, yet the οὐρανός is characterized by movement and has so far to be studied by the physical method.

13 εἰ δὲ μή, ὁμώνυμα. Cf. Arist. *Pol.* 1253ᵃ 20–5 ἀναιρουμένου γὰρ τοῦ ὅλου οὐκ ἔσται ποὺς οὐδὲ χείρ, εἰ μὴ ὁμωνύμως, ὥσπερ εἴ τις λέγει τὴν λιθίνην· διαφθαρεῖσα γὰρ ἔσται τοιαύτη. πάντα δὲ τῷ ἔργῳ ὥρισται καὶ τῇ δυνάμει, ὥστε μηκέτι τοιαῦτα ὄντα οὐ λεκτέον τὰ αὐτὰ εἶναι ἀλλ' ὁμώνυμα; and many similar passages in Aristotle.

COMMENTARY 71

ἆρ' οὖν εἴ γε μηδ' ἐν τοῖς ζῴοις τὴν ζωὴν ἢ ὡδὶ ζητητέον. These 10ᵃ 16 difficult words seem to mean 'if in animals, too, the life does not need explanation, or if it is to be explained, must be explained in this way', i.e. as being their very essence without which they would not be animals at all.

συνάπτει . . . κίνησιν, i. e. the problem of why the heavens 19-20 and the heavenly bodies have movement connects with the problem previously raised about the movement imparted by the ἀκίνητον, in discussing which T. had made the same suggestion, that revolution is of the very essence of the heavens (6ᵃ 7–9).

μηδὲν μάτην, ἄλλως θ' ὁ ἀφορισμός. There is something to be 22 said for Zeller's proposal to read μηδὲν ἄλλως, ὁ ἀφορισμός, treating μάτην as a gloss on ἄλλως. But Usener's emendation is on the whole perhaps better.

πόθεν δ' ἄρξασθαι χρὴ καὶ εἰς ποῖα τελευτᾶν; i. e. with what 24 effects should we begin and to what sort of causes should we assign them?

ἔνια, sc. οὐ ῥᾴδιά ἐστιν ἀφορίζεσθαι. For the ellipse cf. 5ᵃ 27 n. 25

ἢ τίνος αἱ προχωρήσεις. Usener has detected in ll. 4–6 a pretty 10ᵇ 1 evident fragment of an alternative version, and the present clause, the original form of which was no doubt τίνος αἱ προχωρήσεις καὶ ἀναχωρήσεις, is probably an alternative version of that which immediately precedes it.

ἢ . . . μεθισταμένων was detected by Usener to be an alternative 4-5 version of 2–4 ἢ . . . γενέσεις.

εἴ περ μὴ συμβάλλεται. The problem is discussed in Arist. 9 G. A. i. 19.

ἢ ὅλως τριχῶν ἔκφυσις ἔν τισιν τόποις. The purpose of this is 10 discussed in Arist. P. A. 653ᵇ 27–32, 658ᵃ 18–24.

τοῖς οὐκ . . . λελωβημένοις. PJC have τοῖς δὲ καὶ λελωβημένων, 12 RBHD τοῖς δὲ καὶ λελωβημένοις. Only z omits δέ. Usener's τοῖσδε ('by these') καὶ λελωβημένων is not satisfactory. It seems most likely that something like τοῖς οὐκ ὠφελουμένοις has been omitted by haplography, the whole phrase meaning 'in the case of those which are not benefited by the possession of horns, while some have even been injured by them'. Cf. Arist. P. A. 663ᵃ 10 τὸ γὰρ μέγεθος αὐτῶν (sc. τῶν κεράτων) καὶ τὸ πολυσχιδὲς μᾶλλον βλάπτει ἢ ὠφελεῖ (sc. τὰς ἐλάφους).

72 COMMENTARY

10ᵇ 13 παραιωρήσει, 'by being hung up by their horns', *sc.* through these catching on trees and the like.

15 ὥσπερ ὁ ἐρῳδιὸς ὀχεύει. Cf. Arist. *H. A.* 609ᵇ 24–5 (κράζει τε γὰρ καὶ αἷμα, ὥς φασιν, ἀφίησιν ἐκ τῶν ὀφθαλμῶν ὀχεύων), 616ᵇ 33. Aristotle makes this statement only about the variety called πέλλος, *ardea cinerea*, the ash-coloured heron.

καὶ τὸ ἡμερόβιον ζῇ. The name *hemerobion* occurs in Plin. xi. 36 (43). The insect described by Pliny, and probably that referred to by T., is identical with Aristotle's ἐφήμερον, *ephemera longicauda*, the day-fly. Cf. *H. A.* 490ᵃ 34–ᵇ 3, 552ᵇ 17–23, *P. A.* 682ᵃ 26.

20 τούτων χάριν, i.e. for the sake of the animals in question. Usener's τοῦ is an unnecessary emendation.

23 μορφαῖς, εἴδεσιν, δυνάμεσιν are datives of 'respect'. Cf. perhaps 7ᵃ 12 f.

25 μὴ ποιοῦσιν, 'for people who do not make this supposition'. For the construction cf. 11ᵇ 2–5 and Arist. *Met.* 1084ᵃ 9 καίτοι οὔτε κατὰ τὴν θέσιν ἐνδέχεται οὔτε κατὰ λόγον, τάττουσί γ' οὕτω τὰς ἰδέας. Usener's conjecture μὴ προσοῦσαν, 'when a determinate nature is not present', is highly improbable.

11ᵃ 1 εἰ δὲ μή, *sc.* τινος ἕνεκά ἐστι ταῦτα, understood from 10ᵇ 23, 10ᵇ 24–11ᵃ 1 being parenthetical.

9 παραλείπει. παραλείπειν should perhaps be read, this being part of τὰ λεγόμενα (l. 4). But possibly the influence of ὅτι (l. 5) may still cover παραλείπει.

9–11 οἷον ... γάρ. Aristotle explains in *P. A.* 665ᵃ 9–26 that nature puts the windpipe before the gullet because it is more honourable (τιμιώτερον, l. 22) to be before than behind and the heart and lungs, to which the windpipe leads, are more honourable than the stomach, to which the gullet leads.

11–12 καὶ ... τιμιώτατον. Aristotle explains in *P. A.* 667ᵃ 3–6 why the blood is purer in the middle ventricle than in the other two.

13 εἰ γὰρ καὶ ἡ ὄρεξις οὕτως, ἀλλ' κτλ. This is clearly the right punctuation, not Brandis's and Usener's εἰ γάρ, καὶ ἡ ὄρεξις οὕτως. ἀλλ' κτλ.

14 ἐμφαίνει can hardly be taken as intransitive (L. and S. quote no example of this before Cebes, first century A.D.), and we must treat 'the observed facts' as its subject and ἐκεῖνο as its object, or alternatively read ἐμφαίνεται ὅτι.

COMMENTARY

ἀκαριαίου καὶ βέλτιον τὸ εἶναι. The manuscript reading ἀκαριαῖον 11ª 18 καὶ βέλτιον τὸ εἶναι cannot stand. Usener's conjecture of τῷ for τό gives a good sense, 'of living things themselves only a tiny part is better for being alive'. It would be possible to read ἀκαριαῖον, κεἰ βέλτιον, τὸ εἶναι ('the being of living things is momentary, even if it is better'), but the contraction κεἰ is not very probable, and the reading we have printed is perhaps the most likely. In Aristotle ἀκαριαῖος seems always to mean 'tiny' without reference to time.

πολὺ . . . ἀμαθεστάτου. The manuscript readings here are 19-21 corrupt, and Usener's πολὺ δὲ πλῆθος εἰ τοῦ κακοῦ, ἐν ἀοριστίᾳ δὲ μόνον καὶ οἷον ὕλης εἴδει, καθαιρεῖν τὰ τῆς φύσεως ἀμαθεστάτου puts εἰ in an unlikely position and offers in καθαιρεῖν an improbable emendation of καθά περ.

If Sylburg's correction εἰκῇ in l. 22 is (as seems almost certain) right, the sentence beginning there rejects wholesale attacks on the goodness of the universe. And since that sentence is connected with the present sentence by γάρ, the present sentence should fit in with that line of thought. We suppose therefore that, while in this chapter so far T. has been pointing out the limits (11ª 2) to the purposiveness in the universe, he is now, on the other hand, asserting its goodness on the whole (τὸ ὅλον, l. 18)—which is certainly the conclusion of the whole chapter (τὰ μὲν οὖν ὄντα καλῶς ἔτυχεν ὄντα, l. 25). The thought may be compared with that of Arist. *Met.* 1010ª 25–32 ἔτι δ' ἄξιον ἐπιτιμῆσαι τοῖς οὕτως ὑπολαμβάνουσιν, ὅτι καὶ αὐτῶν τῶν αἰσθητῶν ἐπὶ τῶν ἐλαττόνων τὸν ἀριθμὸν ἰδόντες οὕτως ἔχοντα περὶ ὅλου τοῦ οὐρανοῦ ὁμοίως ἀπεφήναντο. ὁ γὰρ περὶ ἡμᾶς τοῦ αἰσθητοῦ τόπος ἐν φθορᾷ καὶ γενέσει διατελεῖ μόνος ὤν· ἀλλ' οὗτος οὐθὲν ὡς εἰπεῖν μόριον τοῦ παντός ἐστιν, ὥστε δικαιότερον ἂν δι' ἐκεῖνα τούτων ἀπεψηφίσαντο ἢ διὰ ταῦτα ἐκείνων κατεψηφίσαντο.

T. can hardly, therefore, be admitting that the good in the universe is as a whole small in amount, and therefore τὸ δ' ὅλον σπάνιόν τι καὶ ἐν ὀλίγοις τὸ ἀγαθόν (ll. 18 f.) cannot express his own view, but should be detached from what precedes and connected with what follows, and become part of the belief which is said to be ἀμαθεστάτου (l. 21). We therefore read a full stop instead of a comma in l. 18, and a comma instead of a full stop in l. 19.

74   COMMENTARY

11ᵃ 20   εἶναι in l. 20 seems to have been first represented by the abbreviation εἰ̑, which survives in RBHD, and then corrupted into ἦ or ἡ.

In οὐκ ἐν ἀοριστίᾳ δὲ μόνον καὶ οἷον ὕλης εἴδει, καθά περ τὰ τῆς φύσεως T. conveys by implication his own opinion that the evil in the universe is not a positive principle but simply due to the indefinite material principle not having been thoroughly shaped to purposive ends—an explanation which, he implies, is adequate to explain whatever evil there is in nature (καθά περ τὰ τῆς φύσεως, l. 21).—The phrase ἐν ὕλης εἴδει is common in Aristotle (e. g. *Met.* 983ᵇ 7).

22   εἰκῇ γὰρ οἱ περὶ τῆς ὅλης οὐσίας λέγοντες κτλ. is perhaps a reminiscence of Aristotle's remark about Anaxagoras, νοῦν δή τις εἰπὼν ἐνεῖναι . . . τὸν αἴτιον τοῦ κόσμου καὶ τῆς τάξεως πάσης οἷον νήφων ἐφάνη παρ' εἰκῇ λέγοντας τοὺς πρότερον (*Met.* 984ᵇ 15-18).

23-5   ὥσπερ . . . ἑκατέρωθεν. The view ascribed here to Speusippus is no doubt connected with the Pythagorean doctrine which placed the world-fire at the centre of the universe (Arist. *De Caelo* 293ᵃ 20-21), on the ground that this was the most honourable position (ib. 27-ᵇ 1). It is well known that Speusippus based his views to a large extent on those of the Pythagoreans, with whom Aristotle occasionally couples him (*Met.* 1072ᵇ 31, *E. N.* 1096ᵇ 5-7). But it is hard to see the connexion between the view here ascribed to him and his doctrine that the good is not a primary principle but something that emerges in the course of evolution (Arist. *Met.* 1072ᵇ 30-34, 1091ᵃ 29-36, 1092ᵃ 11-15).

24   τὰ δ', sc. τὰ μὴ τίμια.

25   τὰ μὲν οὖν ὄντα καλῶς ἔτυχεν ὄντα. μὲν οὖν is corrective as in Arist. *Rhet.* 1399ᵃ 14-15 οὐ τοίνυν δεῖ παιδεύεσθαι· φθονεῖσθαι γὰρ οὐ δεῖ. δεῖ μὲν οὖν παιδεύεσθαι· σοφὸν γὰρ εἶναι δεῖ. μὲν οὖν often has this force in replies in Plato, e.g. *Crito* 44 b 4, *Prot.* 309 d 1, *Gorg.* 466 a 6.

11ᵇ 1   Usener argues for a hiatus between ἐπί and μιμεῖσθαι, and thinks the clause may have read something like . . . μακρὰν τὴν ἀπόστασιν ἐπινοοῦντες τῶν τῇδε ἀποφαίνονται τὸ ἓν μιμεῖσθαί γ' ἐθέλειν ἅπαντα. The word ἐπιμιμεῖσθαι does not seem to be recorded elsewhere, but is quite possible in itself, and it appears much simpler to retain it and merely substitute δ' for γ', both μακρὰν τὴν ἀπόστασιν (sc. εἶναι) and ἐπιμιμεῖσθαι ἐθέλειν ἅπαντα being taken to depend on ποιοῦσι, understood from ποιεῖ, ᵃ 24.

For ἀπόστασιν, used of the gulf between the Platonic orders of 11ᵇ 1 being, cf. Philop. *in De An.* 77. 13-20.

καίτοι... ἑτέρας. A good sense can be assigned to the passage 2-7 with either of the manuscript readings, ὅλως or ὅλως δ', in l. 5. (1) With ὅλως δ' we must take καθά περ ... ἑνός (ll. 2-3) as a principal clause, καθά περ going adverbially with ἀντίθεσίν τινα ποιοῦσιν, 'they make as it were an antithesis', and ποιοῦσιν governing also οὐχ οἷόν τε (*sc.* εἶναι) in l. 5. (2) With ὅλως, it looks at first sight as if we must take καθά περ ... ἑνός as a subordinate clause. But 'just as they make an antithesis between the One and the indefinite dyad, the universe cannot exist without the dyad' is not really good sense, and a better meaning can be got by taking ποιοῦσιν as the dative of the participle; for the construction cf. μὴ ποιοῦσιν, 10ᵇ 25. Then ἰσομοιρεῖν, ὑπερέχειν, and τὰς ἀρχὰς ἐναντίας (*sc.* εἶναι), ll. 6-7, depend on an implicit ἀνάγκη after ἀλλ'.

On the whole it seems most likely that the δ' of the manuscripts other than P in l. 5 is an attempt to emend a construction which was not understood through failure to notice the idiomatic use of the participle ποιοῦσιν.

τῆς ἀορίστου δυάδος καὶ τοῦ ἑνός. Cf. 6ᵃ 24 n., 25 n. 2

ᾗ καὶ τὰς ἀρχὰς ἐναντίας. It seems impossible to make good 7 sense of the manuscript reading ἢ καὶ τὰς ἀρχὰς ἐναντίας. That the ἀρχαί should be contrary is not an alternative to the view already indicated, but is implied in that view. It seems necessary therefore to read ᾗ καί for ἢ καί. Cf. 9ᵇ 1 n. The reading ἢ καί is probably due to ἢ καί in the previous line.

ἐφ' ὅσον ἐνδέχεται. Cf. Arist. *G. A.* 788ᵇ 20-22 τὴν φύσιν ὑπο- 9 τιθέμεθα ... οὔτ' ἐλλείπουσαν οὔτε μάταιον οὐθὲν ποιοῦσαν τῶν ἐνδεχομένων περὶ ἕκαστον.

The insertion of ἐν is confirmed by 8ᵃ 23. 12

τὰ περὶ τὰς τῆς γῆς λεχθέντα μεταβολάς. Cf. 10ᵃ 25-ᵇ 7. 14

τήν γε τάξιν. PJC have τήν τε τάξιν, and Usener *may* be 18 right in conjecturing that καὶ τὸ ὡρισμένον should be added; cf. 6ᵇ 27 τοῖς γὰρ τιμιωτάτοις οἰκειότατον ἡ τάξις καὶ τὸ ὡρίσθαι, Arist. *Met.* 1078ᵃ 36 τοῦ δὲ καλοῦ μέγιστα εἴδη τάξις καὶ συμμετρία καὶ τὸ ὡρισμένον. But it is more likely that τε has arisen, as it often does (cf. 10ᵃ 17), by corruption of γε. The point of γε is that T. ascribes to τὰ οὐράνια and τὰ μαθημα-

11ᵇ 18 τικά order at least, though perhaps not necessarily teleology (l. 15).

19 εἰ μὴ ἄρα καὶ πρότερα τούτων may mean: (1) 'unless indeed there are things even prior to the objects of mathematics', i.e. divine beings or Platonic Forms; or (2) 'unless indeed the objects of mathematics are even prior to the heavenly bodies in respect of orderliness'. The latter rendering seems preferable.

21-3 πλὴν ... ἀτόμων, i.e. unless one supposes, with the Atomists, that the primary mathematical shapes, i.e. the atoms, of which everything is built up, have an indefinite variety of character. For this feature of the Atomistic doctrine cf. Arist. *De Gen. et Corr.* 314ᵃ 21-3, *De Caelo* 303ᵃ 10-12.

24 ἐξ ἀρχῆς ἐλέχθη, ᵃ 1-3.

12ᵃ 4-ᵇ 5 Cf. Introduction, p. ix.

INDEX VERBORUM

* = *apparatus criticus*

ἀγαθός 8ᵇ1, 11ᵃ19
ἄγειν 7ᵇ22, 8ᵃ4, 11
ἄγνωστος 9ᵃ22   ἔνια γνωστὰ τῷ ἄγνωστα εἶναι 9ᵃ19
ἄδεκτος 5ᵇ18
ἀδύνατος 5ᵇ13, 7ᵇ8, 16
ἀεί. μεταδιδόναι τοῦ ἀ. καὶ τοῦ τεταγμένου 11ᵃ7
ἀζήτητος 6ᵃ3
ἀήρ 7ᵇ2, 11ᵇ17
ἀίδιος 9ᵇ24   τὰ ἀίδια 4ᵃ16
αἴσθησις 7ᵇ19, 9ᵇ9   αἱ αἰσθήσεις ἐν ψυχῇ γίνονται 5ᵇ5   ἡ ... αἴ. καὶ τὰς διαφορὰς θεωρεῖ καὶ τὰς αἰτίας ζητεῖ 8ᵇ10
αἰσθητός 4ᵃ7, 20, ᵇ19, 6ᵇ8, 7ᵇ15, 9ᵇ3, 11ᵇ18
αἰτία 5ᵃ22, 7ᵇ19, 8ᵇ11, 9ᵇ11, 11ᵇ8   μέχρι πόσου καὶ τίνων ζητητέον αἰτίας 9ᵇ3
αἴτιος 4ᵇ21, 5ᵃ1, ᵇ7   αἴτιον 9ᵃ2   δι' αἰτίου θεωρεῖν 9ᵇ8
ἀκαριαῖος 11ᵃ18
ἀκίνητος 4ᵃ7, ᵇ22   τὴν ὑπὸ τοῦ ἀκινήτου κίνησιν 10ᵃ20
*ἀκολουθεῖν 8ᵃ2
ἄκρα, τὰ 9ᵇ10, 11ᵃ24
ἀλήθεια 6ᵇ16
ἀληθής 8ᵃ16   ἀληθέστερος 8ᵇ12, 9ᵇ14, 23
ἀληθινώτερος 5ᵃ12
ἀλλοίωσις [10ᵇ4]
ἀλλότριος 9ᵇ5
ἄλογος 7ᵃ10
ἅμα (v. supra, p. xxxii) 5ᵃ12, ᵇ3, 6ᵇ3, 9ᵇ22   cum dativo 5ᵃ25, 6ᵃ8
ἀμαθέστατος 11ᵃ21
ἀμερής 8ᵃ3
ἀμετάβλητος 4ᵃ8
ἀμορφία 11ᵇ4
ἄμορφος 6ᵇ24
ἀμῶς γέ πως 4ᵇ12
ἀνάγειν *7ᵇ22   ἐν τῷ ἀ. εἰς τὰς ἀρχάς 6ᵇ11
ἀναγκαῖος 9ᵇ18
ἀνάγκη 4ᵇ13, 8ᵇ19, 10ᵃ26, ᵇ19, 11ᵇ16   *11ᵃ5
ἀναιρεῖν 9ᵇ5, 21, 11ᵇ11
ἀναλογία 9ᵃ6   κατ' ἀναλογίαν 4ᵇ12, 8ᵃ19, 9ᵃ7, 21
ἀναξήρανσις 10ᵇ2

ἀνάπτειν 6ᵇ13, 7ᵇ11, 13, 11ᵇ8
ἀνάρροια. αἱ ἔφοδοι καὶ ἀνάρροιαι θαλάττης 10ᵇ1
ἀναφέρειν 6ᵃ7
*ἀναχώρησις 10ᵇ2
'Ανδρόνικος in scholio 12ᵃ4
ἀνήνυτον, τὸ 5ᵃ17
ἄνθρωπος 6ᵃ21
ἀντίθεσις. ἀντίθεσίν τινα ... τῆς ἀορίστου δυάδος καὶ τοῦ ἑνός 11ᵇ2
*ἀντικαταλλακτέον 7ᵇ13
ἀντικεῖσθαι 7ᵃ9
ἀντιμεταλλακτέον 7ᵇ13
*ἀξιόλογος (5ᵃ23)
ἀξιόπιστος 7ᵇ18
ἀξιοῦν 5ᵇ15, 6ᵃ3, 16
ἀξιόχρεως cum genetivo 4ᵃ20
ἀόρατον, τὸ 9ᵃ23 (bis)
ἀοριστία 11ᵃ20
ἀόριστος 8ᵃ12   οἱ τὸ ἓν καὶ τὴν ἀόριστον δυάδα ποιοῦντες 6ᵃ24   τὰ μὲν ἀπὸ τῆς ἀορίστου δυάδος 6ᵃ28   τὰς ... ἀρχὰς ἀορίστους εἶναι 7ᵃ19   ἀόριστον τοῖς εἴδεσιν 8ᵃ18   τῆς ἀορίστου δυάδος 11ᵇ2
ἀπαιτεῖν. ἀφορισμὸν ἀπαιτοῦντα 7ᵇ7
ἀπαρτίζειν 8ᵃ5
ἀπάτη 9ᵇ16
ἄπαυστος 5ᵃ3
ἄπειρος *infinitus* 11ᵃ17   ἄπειρον 6ᵇ1, 11ᵇ3   ἡ ... εἰς τὰ ἄ. ὁδός 9ᵇ4
ἀπέχειν 9ᵃ7
ἁπλῶς 4ᵇ20, 5ᵃ9, 8ᵇ13, 9ᵇ7, 10ᵃ9, 11ᵃ3, 4, 5
ἀποδιδόναι 4ᵇ17, 5ᵃ8, 6ᵃ17   ἀποδοτέον 5ᵃ10
ἀπορεῖν 6ᵃ6, 13, ᵇ24, 7ᵇ10
ἀπορία 8ᵃ21, ᵇ13, 10ᵃ20
ἄπορος 5ᵃ23, 9ᵇ2, 10ᵇ24
ἀπόστασις 9ᵇ26, 11ᵇ1
*ἀποφαίνεσθαι 11ᵇ1
ἀπόφασις 5ᵃ13
ἅπτεσθαι 6ᵇ12, 9ᵇ15
ἀπωθεῖν 5ᵇ21
ἀργία 7ᵇ12
ἀριθμός 4ᵇ4, 6ᵃ21, ᵇ2, 14, 8ᵇ26, 9ᵃ5   κατ' ἀριθμόν 4ᵇ8   ὅσοι τοὺς ἀριθμοὺς λέγουσιν 5ᵃ27   τοὺς ἀριθμοὺς φασιν τὸ ἓν 5ᵃ27   τοὺς ... ἀριθμοὺς γεννήσαντες 6ᵃ25
ἄριστος 5ᵇ8, 6ᵃ2, 4, 11ᵃ12   εἰς

78 INDEX VERBORUM

ὄρεξιν... τὴν ἀρίστην 5ᵃ21   τὸ ἄριστον 5ᵇ1   εἰ... τὸ ἄριστον ἀπὸ τοῦ ἀρίστου 5ᵇ26-7   τοῦ... εἰς τὸ ἄριστον 11ᵃ2   τὴν φύσιν (εἰκὸς) ἐν ἅπασιν ὀρέγεσθαι τοῦ ἀρίστου 11ᵃ6   οὐδὲ τὸν θεὸν... δύνασθαι πάντ' εἰς τὸ ἄριστον ἄγειν 11ᵇ9
Ἀριστοτέλης in scholio 12ᵇ2
ἀρκεῖν ⟨5ᵃ23⟩
ἄρρην 10ᵇ8
ἄρτιος 5ᵃ6
ἄρχεσθαι 10ᵃ24
ἀρχή initium 9ᵃ11, 13, 25, ᵇ6, 8, 9 ἁ. (sc. τῆς θεωρίας) 4ᵃ9   κινήσεως ἀρχήν 5ᵇ5   αἱ ἀρχαί (sc. τῆς κινήσεως) πλείους 5ᵃ19   principium 4ᵃ15, ᵇ9, 19, 6ᵃ16, ᵇ14, 16, 17, 21, 22, 7ᵃ13, ᵇ9, 12, 11ᵇ7, 25, 12ᵃ1   τὰ... ὑπὸ τὰς ἀρχάς 4ᵃ16   ἡ πάντων ἀ. 4ᵇ15   ἀρχήν... μίαν πάντων 5ᵃ6   ἐν τῷ ἀνάγειν εἰς τὰς ἀρχάς 6ᵇ12   τὰ μετὰ τὰς ἀρχάς 6ᵇ19, 7ᵃ4   πῶς... χρὴ καὶ ποίας τὰς ἀρχὰς ὑποθέσθαι 6ᵇ23   τὰ... κατὰ τὰς ἀρχάς 7ᵃ6   τὰς... ἀρχὰς ἀορίστους εἶναι 7ᵃ19 *6ᵃ17, 11ᵇ1
Ἀρχύτας 6ᵃ19
ἀσθένεια 5ᵇ14, 9ᵇ12
*ἀστήρ 7ᵃ23
ἀστρολογία 9ᵇ27, 10ᵃ5
*ἀστρολογικός 9ᵇ27
ἀστρολόγος 5ᵃ23
ἀσύνετος 5ᵇ18
ἄτακτον, τὸ 11ᵇ4
ἀτακτότερος 4ᵃ4
ἄτομα, τὰ 11ᵇ23   διαίρεσις εἰς τὰ ἄ. 9ᵃ3
ἄτοπος 5ᵃ18, ᵇ14, 7ᵇ23
αὐτόματον, τὸ 10ᵇ27
αὐτομάτως 7ᵃ18
ἀφαιρεῖν 6ᵃ12, 13   ἀφαιρετέον 5ᵃ11
ἀφανής 5ᵃ17
ἀφορίζειν 4ᵃ2, 9ᵃ25, 10ᵃ19
ἀφορισμός 7ᵇ6, 10ᵃ23
ἄψυχον. ἄπειρον... τὸ ἄ. 11ᵃ17   ἄψυχα 7ᵃ17, 9ᵃ15, 10ᵇ21

βελτίων 7ᵇ11   τὸ βέλτιον 8ᵃ14, 11ᵇ15   σχεδὸν ἰσομοιρεῖ τὸ χεῖρον τῷ βελτίονι 8ᵃ24   ὅπου... οἷόν τε τὸ β., ἐνταῦθα οὐδαμοῦ παραλείπει 11ᵃ9   αὐτῶν τῶν ἐμψύχων ἀκαριαίου καὶ β. τὸ εἶναι 11ᵃ18   τῆς εἰς τὸ β. ὁρμῆς 11ᵇ27
βία 10ᵇ14
βλέπειν 9ᵇ13
βούλεσθαι 6ᵃ2

γαίη 5ᵇ17
γένεσις 8ᵃ12, 10ᵇ4, 18   κατὰ τὴν γένεσιν 6ᵇ15   ζῴων καὶ φυτῶν καὶ καρπῶν γενέσεις 7ᵇ5
γεννᾶν. τοὺς... ἀριθμοὺς γεννήσαντες 6ᵃ25   γεννῶντος τοῦ ἡλίου 7ᵇ5
γένος 8ᵇ20, 9ᵃ5, 15   κατὰ γ. 4ᵇ8
γῆ 6ᵇ26, 7ᵇ2, 10ᵃ28, [ᵇ4]   τὰ περὶ τὰς τῆς γῆς λεχθέντα μεταβολὰς 11ᵇ14
γίνεσθαι 8ᵃ26   τὸ μὴ... γεγονός 8ᵇ7
γνωστός. ἔνια γνωστὰ τῷ ἄγνωστα εἶναι 9ᵃ19
*γνωτός 9ᵃ19
γραμματική 7ᵃ2
γραμμή 8ᵇ26

δεικνύναι 9ᵇ27
δέχεσθαι 6ᵃ1, 11ᵃ15
δηλοῦν 6ᵃ28
Δημόκριτος 11ᵇ22
διαιρεῖν 9ᵃ18, 24
διαίρεσις 9ᵃ6, 20   δ. εἰς τὰ ἄτομα 9ᵃ2
διαιρετός 5ᵃ8   τὸ διαιρετόν 5ᵃ11
διαμένειν 4ᵇ16
διάνοια. ἡ τῆς διανοίας (sc. κίνησις) 5ᵇ9   ὑποβάλλει (sc. ἡ αἴσθησις) τῇ διανοίᾳ 8ᵇ13
διατιθέναι 6ᵃ20   *6ᵇ7
διαφέρειν 8ᵇ19
διαφορά 6ᵃ5, 8ᵇ11, 17, 9ᵃ17, 11ᵃ1   τὸ ἐπίστασθαι... οὐκ ἄνευ διαφορᾶς τινος 8ᵇ16
διικνεῖσθαι 5ᵇ13
*δισταγμός 11ᵃ4
δισταμός 11ᵃ4
δυάς. οἱ τὸ ἓν καὶ τὴν ἀόριστον δυάδα ποιοῦντες 6ᵃ25   τὰ μὲν ἀπὸ τῆς ἀορίστου δυάδος 6ᵇ1   ἀντίθεσίν τινα... τῆς ἀορίστου δυάδος καὶ τοῦ ἑνός 11ᵇ3
δυναμικός 6ᵇ25
δύναμις 4ᵇ14, 5ᵃ1, 7ᵃ12, 8ᵃ10, 19, 10ᵇ23
δύνασθαι 5ᵇ28, 9ᵇ8, 11, 11ᵇ8

ἐγώ 9ᵃ8   ἡμῖν opp. ἁπλῶς 9ᵇ6
ἐθέλειν 11ᵇ1
εἰδέναι 9ᵇ22   ποσαχῶς τὸ εἰ. 9ᵃ24
εἶδος 8ᵇ20, 9ᵃ5, 10ᵃ4, ᵇ23, 11ᵃ21   κατ' εἶδος 4ᵇ8   ἀόριστον τοῖς εἴδεσιν 8ᵃ18
εἰκῇ 7ᵃ14, 11ᵃ22
εἰκός ⟨11ᵃ5⟩
εἰκότως 7ᵇ10
εἶναι. τὸ ὄν 8ᵇ5   τὸ μὴ ὄν 8ᵇ7

INDEX VERBORUM 79

τὸ . . . ὂν ὅτι πολλαχῶς, φανερόν 8^b 10   τὰ ὄντα 6^b 17, 8^a 9, 11^a 25, 12^a 2   τὸ εἶ. 8^a 15, ^b 2, 11^a 18
εἶς. μία τις κατ' ἀριθμόν 4^b 7   ἀρχὴν . . . μίαν πάντων 5^a 7   εἴτε . . . ἓν τὸ κινοῦν 5^a 18   ὅσοι . . . τὸ ἕν . . . λέγουσιν 5^a 26   τοὺς ἀριθμούς φασιν τὸ ἕν 5^a 28   οἱ τὸ ἓν καὶ τὴν ἀόριστον δυάδα ποιοῦντες 6^a 24   τοῦ ἑνός 6^b 2   ἀντίθεσίν τινα . . . τῆς ἀορίστου δυάδος καὶ τοῦ ἑνός 11^b 3   *11^b 1
ἕκαστον. τὸ καθ' ἕ. 10^a 11   ἕκαστα 7^a 17, 20, 9^a 10
ἑκατέρωθεν 11^a 25
ἔκφυσις 10^b 10
ἔλαφος 10^b 12
ἐλάχιστον, τό.   κατὰ τοὐλάχιστον 7^a 16
ἔμμορφος 7^a 6, 8
ἐμποιεῖν 4^b 3
ἔμπροσθεν 11^a 10
ἐμφαίνειν 4^b 12, 8^b 15, 11^a 14
ἔμψυχος 5^b 2   ὀλίγον . . . τι τὸ ἔμψυχον 11^a 16   ἔμψυχα 7^a 17   αὐτῶν τῶν ἐμψύχων ἀκαριαίον καὶ βέλτιον τὸ εἶναι 11^a 17   *5^b 6
ἐναντίος 6^b 18, 11^b 7   ἐναντία plur. 8^a 23, ^b 5   τὴν ὅλην οὐσίαν ἐξ ἐναντίων . . . καὶ (ἐν) ἐναντίοις οὖσαν 11^b 11-12
ἐνδέχεσθαι 7^b 20, 9^a 21, 11^a 6   ἐφ' ὅσον ἐνδέχεται 11^b 10
ἕνεκα. τὸ ἕνεκά του 7^a 21, 11^a 1, ^b 27
ἐνεργάζεσθαι 8^b 14
ἐνέργεια 5^a 7, ^b 23, 7^b 13, 8^a 11, 9^a 4, 10^a 11
ἐνεργεῖν 10^a 12
ἐντιμότατα, τὰ 5^b 22
ἐξαίρειν 5^a 9
ἐπεισοδιώδης. μὴ ἐπεισοδιῶδες τὸ πᾶν 4^a 14
ἕπεσθαι. (τὰ) ἑπόμενα 9^a 14
ἐπί. κατ' ἀναλογίαν ληπτέον ἐ. τὰς τέχνας 8^a 20
ἐπιζητεῖν 5^b 11
ἐπιθεωρεῖσθαι 11^b 13
ἐπιμιμεῖσθαι 11^b 1
*ἐπινοεῖν 11^b 1
ἐπίπεδον. τὰ ἐπίπεδα (sc. γεννήσαντες) 6^a 26
ἐπιποθεῖν 8^a 8
ἐπιπρόσθησις 10^b 13
ἐπίστασθαι 9^a 4   τὸ ἐ. . . . οὐκ ἄνευ διαφορᾶς τινος 8^b 16   πλεοναχῶς . . . ὄντος τοῦ ἐ. 9^b 10   τί τὸ ἐ. 9^a 26   *9^b 1
ἐπιστήμη 6^b 20   σχεδὸν . . . ἐ. πᾶσα

τῶν ἰδίων 8^b 20   τὸ ἐν πλείοσιν τὸ αὐτὸ συνιδεῖν ἐπιστήμης 8^b 25
*ἐργάζεσθαι 8^b 14
Ἕρμιππος in scholio 12^a 4
ἐρύειν 5^b 17
ἔρχεσθαι 6^a 23
ἐρῳδιός 10^b 15
ἐσθλά 8^a 27
Ἑστιαῖος 6^b 10
ἔσχατος 9^a 14
*ἔτειος 7^b 3
ἐτήσιος. τὰς ὥρας τὰς ἐτησίους 7^b 3
εὖ. πολὺ τὸ οὐχ ὑπακοῦον οὐδὲ δεχόμενον τὸ εὖ 11^a 15
εὐλόγως 6^b 21
εὐλογώτερος 4^a 13, ^b 8
Εὐριπίδης 8^a 26
Εὔρυτος 6^a 20
εὔσημος 4^a 19
ἐφάπτεσθαι 6^a 27
ἐφεξῆς. τὰ ἐ. . . . ἀποδιδόναι 6^a 17
ἔφεσις 5^a 15   ἡ ἔ. . . . μετὰ ψυχῆς 5^a 28   ἐφέσει τινὶ καὶ ὀρέξει 6^a 9
ἐφετικός. διὰ τί τὰ κυκλικὰ μόνον ἐφετικά 5^b 11
ἔφοδος. αἱ ἔφοδοι καὶ ἀνάρροιαι θαλάττης 10^a 28

Ζεύς 5^b 16
ζῆν 10^b 15
ζητεῖν 5^a 22, ^b 19, 7^b 6, 19, 8^a 22, ^b 1, 11, 13, 15, 9^a 21, 23, 10^b 24   ζητητέον 9^b 3, 10^a 17
ζήτησις 6^b 22
ζωή 4^b 3, 10^a 17   ζ. γὰρ τοῖς ἔχουσιν (sc. ἡ ψυχή) 5^b 3   οἷον . . . ζ. τις ἡ περιφορὰ τοῦ παντός 10^a 16
ζῷον 5^b 5, 7^a 22, 8^a 5, ^b 27, 9^a 14, 10^a 5, 13, 17, 11^a 8   ζῴων . . . γενέσεις 7^b 4   ἐν αὐτοῖς τοῖς ζῴοις τὰ μὲν ὥσπερ μάταια 10^b 7   τὰς τροφὰς καὶ γενέσεις τῶν ζῴων 10^b 18

ἤ εἰ syn. πλὴν εἰ 5^a 5
*ἡγεῖσθαι 9^b 1
ἥλιος 7^b 5
ἡμερόβιον 10^b 15
Ἡράκλειτος 7^a 15
ἠρεμεῖν 7^b 16, 8^a 1, 10^a 15
ἠρεμία 5^a 24, 7^b 10

θάλασσα 5^b 17
θάλαττα. αἱ ἔφοδοι καὶ ἀνάρροιαι θαλάττης 10^b 1
θεῖος 4^b 15   τὰ θεῖα 6^b 9   θειότερος 5^a 10   θειότατος 6^a 1

INDEX VERBORUM

θεός 4ᵇ15, 7ᵇ23, 11ᵇ8   οὐδὲ τὸν θεὸν
 . . . δύνασθαι πάντ' εἰς τὸ ἄριστον
 ἄγειν 11ᵇ8
Θεόφραστος in scholio 12ᵇ1, 3
θέσις 10ᵃ3
θεωρεῖν 8ᵇ11, 22   δι' αἰτίου θ. 9ᵇ9
θεωρία 9ᵇ15   τὴν ὑπὲρ τῶν πρώτων
 θεωρίαν 4ᵃ3   ἡ . . . τῶν πρώτων
 (sc. θ.) 4ᵃ5   τῆς τοῦ σύμπαντος
 θεωρίας 12ᵃ1
θῆλυς 10ᵇ9
θιγγάνειν 9ᵇ15
θρίξ 10ᵇ10

ἰδέα 6ᵇ13, 10ᵇ28
ἰδίᾳ 8ᵇ26
ἴδιος 8ᵇ22, 9ᵃ16, 20   τὸ ἴδιον 4ᵇ21
 σχεδὸν . . . ἐπιστήμη πᾶσα τῶν ἰδίων
 8ᵇ21   *10ᵇ28
*ἱκανός 5ᵃ23
ἱκανῶς 9ᵃ18
ἵππος 6ᵃ22
ἰσομοιρεῖν 8ᵃ24, 11ᵇ6
ἰσχυρότερος 5ᵇ15, 6ᵇ19
ἴσως caute asseverantis 4ᵇ13, 8ᵃ3

καθά περ explicative 4ᵇ3, 11ᵇ2
καθόλου 8ᵃ26, ᵇ25, 9ᵃ1, 27   ἐν . . .
 τοῖς κ. 8ᵇ18   τῶν ὑπὸ τὰ κ. 8ᵇ19
 τὰ κ. 8ᵇ20
κακόν, τὸ 11ᵃ20
καλλίων 5ᵇ27   κάλλιστος 7ᵃ15
καρδία. ἐν τῇ μέσῃ κοιλίᾳ τῆς καρδίας
 τὴν κρᾶσιν ἀρίστην 11ᵃ11
καρπύς. καρπῶν γενέσεις 7ᵃ4
*κατάγειν 6ᵇ14
κατακολουθεῖν 11ᵇ16
κατάλοιπος 9ᵇ27
καταπαύειν 6ᵃ23
κενόν 6ᵇ1
κέρας 10ᵇ11
κίνδυνος 7ᵇ17
κινεῖν 4ᵇ23, 5ᵃ5 (bis), ᵇ2, 7ᵇ16, 17, 20,
 21, 10ᵃ12   εἴτε . . . ἓν τὸ κινοῦν
 5ᵃ18   τὰ . . . πρῶτα κινοῦντα 10ᵃ1
 τὸ . . . κινεῖσθαι καὶ ἁπλῶς τῆς φύσεως οἰκεῖον καὶ μάλιστα τοῦ οὐρανοῦ
 10ᵃ9
κίνησις 4ᵇ4, 20, 22, 5ᵃ5, 25, 6ᵃ13,
 7ᵇ12, 14   ψυχῇ . . . ἅμα δοκεῖ
 καὶ κ. ὑπάρχειν 5ᵇ3   τὴν ὑπὸ
 τοῦ ἀκινήτου κίνησιν 10ᵃ20   *5ᵃ3
κινητός 5ᵇ12   τὰ κινητά 9ᵃ12
κνῆσις 10ᵇ13
κοιλία 11ᵃ11
κοινῇ 8ᵇ25
κοινός 9ᵃ27
κοινωνία 4ᵃ10

κόσμος mundus 6ᵇ8, 7ᵃ15   ornatus
 11ᵃ13
κρᾶσις 11ᵃ12
κρείττων 4ᵇ6, 5ᵃ1, 9, ᵇ8
κυκλική (sc. κίνησις) 5ᵃ3, ᵇ23   εἰ
 . . . τῆς κυκλικῆς αἴτιον τὸ πρῶτον
 5ᵇ7
κυκλικός. τῆς κυκλικῆς περιφορᾶς 5ᵇ24
 τὰ κυκλικά 5ᵃ16   διὰ τί τὰ κυκλικὰ
 μόνον ἐφετικά 5ᵇ11
κυκλοφορία 5ᵇ28
*κυριώτερος 10ᵃ7   κυριώτατος 4ᵇ5
 τὰ κυριώτατα 10ᵃ7
κωλύειν 5ᵇ28, 6ᵃ11

λαμβάνειν 4ᵇ14, 5ᵇ23, 7ᵃ16, 9ᵃ27,
 ᵇ9, 10ᵇ16, 28, 11ᵇ22, 25   ληπτέον
 8ᵃ3, 20, 11ᵃ2
λέγειν. τοῖς πλεοναχῶς λεγομένοις
 9ᵇ1
λευκά, τὰ 8ᵇ3
*λογοειδής 7ᵇ18
λόγος 5ᵃ6, 12, 14, 22, 6ᵃ15, 7ᵃ12,
 20, ᵇ9, 8ᵃ8, 27, 10ᵇ25, 26   οἱ
 . . . ἁπάντων ζητοῦντες λόγον ἀναιροῦσιν λόγον 9ᵇ21-22   definitio
 8ᵃ14   arith. 4ᵃ23
λογώδης 7ᵇ18
λοιπός 5ᵃ1, ᵇ18, 6ᵇ22, 7ᵃ1   τὰ
 λοιπά 6ᵇ4
λύειν 5ᵃ4
λωβᾶσθαι 10ᵇ12

μαθήματα 9ᵃ17
μαθηματικός 7ᵃ3   μαθηματικά 6ᵇ9
 τὰ μαθηματικά 4ᵃ18, 9ᵃ16, 11ᵇ20
μαστός 10ᵇ8
μάταιος. ἐν αὐτοῖς τοῖς ζῴοις τὰ μὲν
 ὥσπερ μάταια 10ᵇ8
μάτην 10ᵃ22
μέγας 9ᵇ17   μείζων 4ᵃ9, 5ᵃ22, 7ᵇ
 18   μέγιστος 7ᵇ2, 9ᵃ11, ᵇ19,
 10ᵇ17
μέγεθος 9ᵇ26, 10ᵇ11
μεθίστασθαι [10ᵇ5]
μέθοδος 6ᵇ18
μέλανα. τὰ λευκὰ καὶ μ. 8ᵇ4
μέλλειν. τὸ μὴ . . . μέλλον 8ᵇ7
μέν om. τὰ μὲν . . . τὰ δ' . . . καὶ
 (καὶ τὰ μὲν J rec.) . . . τὰ δ' 4ᵃ15
μερίς 5ᵃ10
μερισμός 8ᵃ9
μεριστός 5ᵃ11   τὰ μεριστά 8ᵃ6
μέρος 5ᵇ20 (bis), 21 (bis), 7ᵃ11, 10ᵃ4
 ἐν μέρει opp. καθόλου 9ᵃ2
μέσος 11ᵃ11   διὰ τί . . . τῶν . . . περὶ
 τὸ μ. οὐθὲν (sc. ἐφετικόν) 5ᵇ12   τὸ μ.

INDEX VERBORUM 81

τιμιώτατον 11ᵃ12   τὴν τοῦ μέσου χώραν 11ᵃ24
Μετὰ τὰ φυσικά. τῶν Ἀριστοτέλους Μ. τ. φ. in scholio 12ᵇ2
μεταβαίνειν 9ᵇ10
μετάβασις. εἰς τὸ χεῖρον ἡ μ. 7ᵇ8 εἰς... τὸ βέλτιον... ἡ μ. 8ᵃ15
μεταβολή 7ᵃ23, 10ᵇ3, [5] μεταβολὰς ἔχουσα παντοίας 4ᵃ5 καὶ εἰς τοὺς τόπους καὶ εἰς ἄλληλα τὰς μεταβολὰς 5ᵇ26   τὰ περὶ τὰς τῆς γῆς λεχθέντα μεταβολάς 11ᵇ14
μεταδιδόναι 11ᵃ7
μεταδιωκτέον 9ᵃ11
μεταφορά. καθ' ὁμοιότητα καὶ μεταφορὰν 5ᵇ2
μηχανᾶσθαι 4ᵃ21
μιμεῖσθαι 7ᵃ5, 8ᵃ1 *11ᵇ1
μίμησις 5ᵃ25
μνεία 6ᵇ5
μορφή 4ᵃ22, 7ᵃ12, 23, 8ᵃ9, 10ᵇ23, 11ᵇ22
μορφοῦσθαι 6ᵇ26, 8ᵃ13
μουσική 7ᵃ2

Νικόλαος in scholio 12ᵇ2
νοητά 6ᵇ8, 9ᵃ12, ᵇ4   ἐν νοητοῖς... αὐτὴν (sc. τὴν τῶν πρώτων θεωρίαν) τιθέασιν 4ᵃ7   κοινωνία πρὸς ἄλληλα τοῖς τε νοητοῖς καὶ τοῖς τῆς φύσεως 4ᵃ11 εἰ... ἐν τοῖς μαθηματικοῖς μόνον τὰ ν. 4ᵃ19
νομίζειν 4ᵃ9
νοῦς 7ᵇ23, 9ᵇ14

Ξενοκράτης 6ᵇ7

ὁδός. ἡ... εἰς τὸ ἄπειρον ὁ. 9ᵇ4
*οἴεσθαι 11ᵇ1
οἰκεῖος 9ᵃ11, 10ᵃ10   οἰκειότερος 9ᵃ21   οἰκειότατος 6ᵇ28
οἷον explicative 4ᵃ10, 14, 21, 5ᵃ6, ᵇ21, 24, 6ᵃ2, ᵇ20, 25, 7ᵃ9, ᵇ5, 8ᵇ8, 9ᵇ15, 10ᵃ15, 11ᵃ21, ᵇ6
οἷός τε 8ᵇ5, 9ᵃ27, 11ᵃ8-9, ᵇ5
οἰσοφάγος 11ᵃ10
ὅλος. ὁ ὅ. οὐρανός 8ᵃ6   ἡ ὅλη οὐσία 8ᵃ23, 11ᵃ22, ᵇ11   τῇ τοῦ ὅλου περιφορᾷ 10ᵇ28   τὴν τοῦ ὅλου φύσιν 11ᵇ5   τὸ ὅλον adv. 4ᵃ8, 11ᵃ18
ὅλως universe 4ᵃ20, 8ᵃ19, ᵇ24, 10ᵇ2, 10   prorsus 11ᵇ5
Ὅμηρος 5ᵇ15
ὄμμα 10ᵇ14
ὁμογενής 9ᵃ17
ὅμοιος 6ᵃ4, 8ᵇ1, 3

ὁμοιότης 8ᵃ20   καθ' ὁμοιότητα καὶ μεταφορὰν 5ᵇ1
ὁμοίως 5ᵃ26, 6ᵇ8, 7ᵃ4, 16, 8ᵃ3, 9ᵇ3, 11ᵃ8 *8ᵇ24
ὁμοίωσις. κατ' ἄλλην ὁμοίωσιν 4ᵇ13
ὁμώνυμος 10ᵃ13, 15
*ὑρατός 9ᵃ23
ὄργανον 7ᵃ5
ὁρέγεσθαι 6ᵃ10, 8ᵃ1, 11ᵃ6
ὀρεκτόν, τὸ 5ᵃ2
ὄρεξις 11ᵃ14   εἰς ὄρεξιν... τὴν ἀρίστην 5ᵃ20   φυσικὴν ὄρεξιν 5ᵃ24   ἀφ' ἧς (sc. τῆς ψυχῆς) αἱ ὀρέξεις πρὸς ἕκαστον 5ᵇ4   ἀφ' ἧς (sc. τῆς διανοίας) καὶ ἡ ὄ. 5ᵇ10   ἐφίεσθαί τινι καὶ ὀρέξει 6ᵃ9   ἀφελόντα τὴν ὄρεξιν 6ᵃ12
ὁρίζεσθαι 6ᵇ27, 28, 10ᵇ22   ἡ... τῶν πρώτων (sc. θεωρία) ὡρισμένη 4ᵃ6   ὡρισμέναι... ἑκάστων αἱ φύσεις 7ᵃ17 *11ᵇ18
ὁρμή. τῆς εἰς τὸ βέλτιον ὁρμῆς 11ᵇ27
ὅρος 9ᵇ20, 11ᵃ2, ᵇ25
οὐράνια, τὰ 10ᵃ18, 27   μάλιστα... ἂν δόξειεν ἔχειν τὴν γε τάξιν τῶν... αἰσθητῶν τὰ οὐ. 11ᵇ19
οὐρανός 5ᵇ20, 6ᵃ14, ᵇ3, 4, 7ᵃ11, 9ᵇ24, 10ᵃ14, 18   τὸν πρῶτον οὐρανόν 6ᵃ7   ὁ ὅλος οὐ. 8ᵃ6   τὸ... κινεῖσθαι... οἰκεῖον... τοῦ οὐρανοῦ 10ᵃ10
οὐσία syn. τί ἦν εἶναι 5ᵃ8, 6ᵃ7, 8ᵃ13, 9ᵃ5, 10ᵃ11, 14   ἤ τε... οὐ. καὶ τὸ τί ἦν εἶναι καθ' ἕκαστον ἴδιον 8ᵇ21   τὴν πᾶσαν οὐσίαν 4ᵃ13   οἷον ἐξ ἀντικειμένων τὴν ἅπασαν οὐσίαν 7ᵃ10: cf. 8ᵃ23, 11ᵇ11   ἡ τοῦ σύμπαντος οὐ. 10ᵃ3, 11ᵇ26   τῆς ὅλης οὐσίας 11ᵃ22   οὐ. προτέρα καὶ κρείττων (sc. τῶν μαθηματικῶν) 4ᵇ6
ὀχεύειν 10ᵇ15

πάλιν αὖ 7ᵃ20
πᾶν 4ᵃ21   μὴ ἐπεισοδιῶδες τὸ π. 4ᵃ14   ἡ ὅλη... οὐσία τοῦ παντὸς 8ᵃ23   τὴν τοῦ παντὸς φύσιν 8ᵇ8   οἷον... ζωή τις ἡ περιφορὰ τοῦ παντός 10ᵃ16 *11ᵇ26   πάντα 10ᵃ22   ἀρχήν... μίαν πάντων 5ᵃ7   ἄτοπον τὸ μὴ πάντα τὴν αὐτήν (sc. κινεῖσθαι κίνησιν) 5ᵃ18   ἡ πάντων ἀρχή 4ᵇ15
παντοῖος 7ᵇ1   μεταβολὰς ἔχουσα παντοίας 4ᵃ5
παράδειγμα 7ᵇ2
παράδοξος 8ᵇ6   παραδοξότερος 8ᵇ4
παραίρεσις 10ᵇ13

82 INDEX VERBORUM

παραλείπειν 6ᵃ27, 11ᵃ9
παρόμοιος 10ᵇ6
πάσχειν 5ᵇ6   ποιεῖν καὶ π. 7ᵇ21-2
παύεσθαι 6ᵃ8, 18
πειρᾶσθαι 6ᵇ9   πειρατέον 4ᵇ7, 12, 9ᵃ24, 11ᵇ25
πειστικωτέρως 4ᵇ18
περιεργία 8ᵃ22
περίοδος 7ᵃ13
περιτιθέναι 4ᵃ23, 6ᵇ7, 7ᵃ20
περιττύς 4ᵇ10
περιφορά 10ᵃ14   τῆς κυκλικῆς περιφορᾶς 5ᵇ25   ἡ π. (sc. τοῦ πρώτου οὐρανοῦ) 6ᵃ7   οἷον . . . ζωή τις ἡ π. τοῦ παντός 10ᵃ16   τῇ τοῦ ὅλου περιφορᾷ 10ᵇ28
*πιστικωτέρως 4ᵇ18
πίστις 9ᵇ17
πιστύς 10ᵇ27
Πλάτων 6ᵇ11   Π. . . . καὶ οἱ Πυθαγόρειοι 11ᵃ27
πλείων 4ᵇ11, 5ᵃ14, 15, 19, 6ᵇ4, 7ᵇ8, 8ᵃ25, ᵇ6, 18, 24, 10ᵃ28, 11ᵃ16, ᵇ21   ἐπὶ πλέον 8ᵇ16   πλεῖστος 9ᵃ7   πλεῖστον adv. 9ᵃ8
πλεονάκις 10ᵃ24
πλεοναχῶς 9ᵃ10   τοῖς π. λεγομένοις 9ᵇ1
πλῆθος 11ᵃ19   τὸ . . . κατὰ τὸ π. τῶν σφαιρῶν 5ᵃ21
πλὴν εἰ 7ᵃ22-3
ποιεῖν καὶ πάσχειν 7ᵇ21-2
ποιητά 9ᵃ3
ποικιλία 7ᵇ1
ποιός 8ᵃ18
πόλις 8ᵃ5
πολλαχῶς 8ᵇ10   *9ᵇ1
*πολυσχιδέστερος 4ᵃ3
πολυχούστερος 4ᵃ3
πομφύλυξ 7ᵃ22
ποσαχῶς 9ᵃ24
ποσύς 5ᵃ8, 8ᵃ18
πραγματεία. τὰς καθ' ἕκαστα πραγματείας 9ᵇ18
πρακτά, τά 9ᵃ3
προαιρεῖσθαι 11ᵇ10
προβαίνειν 8ᵇ14
προέρχεσθαι 6ᵃ18
πρόεσις 10ᵇ9
προσκαταριθμεῖν 8ᵇ7
πρότερος 4ᵃ15, ᵇ6, 5ᵃ2, 7ᵇ14, 9ᵇ21, 10ᵃ7, ᵇ26, 11ᵇ19   πρότερον adv. 5ᵇ19   πρῶτος 4ᵇ5, 10, 11, 5ᵇ9, 6ᵃ1, 7ᵇ9, 17, 9ᵃ25   τὸν πρῶτον οὐρανόν 6ᵃ6   τὸ πρῶτον primum mobile 5ᵇ27   εἰ . . . τῆς κυκλικῆς αἴτιον τὸ πρῶτον 5ᵇ8   οὐ διικνουμένου τοῦ πρώτου 5ᵇ14   τὰ . . .

πρῶτα κινοῦντα 10ᵃ1   πρῶτα 6ᵇ11, 9ᵃ12, ᵇ10, 11ᵇ13   τὴν ὑπὲρ τῶν πρώτων θεωρίαν 4ᵃ3   ἡ . . . τῶν πρώτων (sc. θεωρία) 4ᵃ5   τοῖς πρώτοις . . . τῆς φύσεως 10ᵃ6
προχώρησις [10ᵇ1]
Πυθαγόρειοι. Πλάτων . . . καὶ οἱ Π. 11ᵃ27
πῦρ 6ᵇ25
πώγων 10ᵇ10

ῥᾴδιος 4ᵇ17, 9ᵇ2, 10ᵃ23

σάρμα 7ᵃ14
*σάρξ 7ᵃ14
*σάρον 7ᵃ14
σαφεστέρως 4ᵇ17
σεμνότερος 4ᵃ8
σκέψις 7ᵇ6
σοφία 8ᵇ9
σπάνιος 11ᵃ18, 23
Σπεύσιππος 11ᵃ23   οἱ περὶ Σπεύσιππον 6ᵇ6
στέρησις. σ. τις κινήσεως 7ᵇ12
συμβαίνειν 6ᵇ17, 7ᵃ23, 11ᵇ11   *5ᵇ23   κατὰ συμβεβηκός 5ᵇ24, 6ᵃ9, 8ᵇ23
συμβάλλεσθαι 10ᵇ9
σύμπαν, τό. ἡ τοῦ σύμπαντος οὐσία 10ᵃ3, 11ᵇ26   τῆς τοῦ σύμπαντος θεωρίας 12ᵃ1
σύμπτωμα 10ᵇ19
συμπτωματικῶς 10ᵃ26
σύμφυτος 6ᵃ10
σύμφωνος 8ᵃ4   τὸ σύμφωνον 5ᵃ20
συνάγειν 7ᵃ21
συνακολουθεῖν 7ᵃ3, 8ᵃ2
συνάπτειν 4ᵇ2, 19, 10ᵃ19
συναυδᾶν 7ᵇ20
συναφή 4ᵃ9, 14, 20
συνεργεῖν 4ᵃ12, 10ᵃ6
σύνεσις 9ᵇ17
συνεχής 5ᵃ3
συνορᾶν 8ᵇ24
σφαῖρα. τὸ . . . κατὰ τὸ πλῆθος τῶν σφαιρῶν 5ᵃ22
σχεδόν 6ᵃ26, 7ᵃ1, 8ᵃ24, ᵇ20
σχῆμα 4ᵃ22, 9ᵇ26
σῶμα. τὰ σώματα (sc. γεννήσαντες) 6ᵃ26
*σωρός 7ᵃ14

τάξις 6ᵇ28, 7ᵃ12, 23   μάλιστα . . . ἂν δόξειεν ἔχειν τὴν γε τάξιν τῶν . . . αἰσθητῶν τὰ οὐράνια 11ᵇ18
τάττειν. μέχρι πόσου τὸ τεταγμένον 7ᵇ7   μεταδιδόναι τοῦ ἀεὶ καὶ τοῦ τεταγμένου 11ᵃ7   τὸ τεταγμένον 11ᵇ21

τέλεος 6ᵃ19, 8ᵇ27   τὸ τέλεον 7ᵃ9
τελεώτερος 6ᵇ20   τελεώτατος 8ᵃ7
τελευτᾶν 10ᵃ25
τέλος 9ᵃ1, ᵇ7
τέχνη 7ᵃ4, 8ᵃ12, 20
τί ἦν εἶναι. ἥ τε ... οὐσία καὶ τὸ τ.
ἡ. εἶ. καθ' ἕκαστον ἴδιον 8ᵇ22
τιθέναι 4ᵃ7, ᵇ5, 6ᵃ17   θετέον 4ᵇ21,
11ᵃ3
Τίμαιος dialogus 6ᵇ27
τίμιον, τὸ 11ᵃ23   τιμιώτερος 7ᵇ14,
10ᵇ26, 11ᵃ10   τιμιώτατος 11ᵃ12
τὰ τιμιώτατα 6ᵇ28
τίς. τὸ τίνος ἕνεκα 10ᵃ1
τόδε syn. οὐσία. τὸ μήτε τ. μήτε ποιὸν
μήτε ποσόν 8ᵃ17
τόπος 6ᵇ1, 10ᵇ11   καὶ εἰς τοὺς
τόπους καὶ εἰς ἄλληλα τὰς μεταβολὰς
5ᵇ25
τρόπος 9ᵃ12, 20, 23, 10ᵃ8   τρόπον
τινά adv. 5ᵃ16, 7ᵇ19, 9ᵇ6   τρόπον τινὰ ἀφωρισμένον adv. 10ᵃ19
τροφή 10ᵇ17
τυγχάνειν 6ᵃ22, 11ᵃ25, ᵇ14

ὑγρότης 10ᵇ2
ὕλη 7ᵃ8, 8ᵃ9, 11ᵃ21
ὑλικός 7ᵃ7
ὑπακούειν. πολὺ τὸ οὐχ ὑπακοῦον οὐδὲ
δεχόμενον τὸ εὖ 11ᵃ15
ὑπάρχειν 5ᵇ3, 6ᵃ11, 8ᵃ16, 17
ὑπεναντίος 5ᵃ16
ὑπέρ syn. περί 4ᵃ2, 6ᵃ13, 10ᵃ22
ὑπερβατός 6ᵃ3, 8ᵇ9
ὑπερέχειν 11ᵇ6
ὑπεροχή 4ᵇ14
ὑποβαίνειν 10ᵃ3
ὑποβάλλειν. ὑποβάλλει (sc. ἡ αἴσθησις)
τῇ διανοίᾳ 8ᵇ12
ὑποκείμενον, τὸ 9ᵃ9
ὑπολαμβάνειν 9ᵇ24
ὑποτιθέναι 6ᵇ23, 11ᵇ22
ὕστερος 4ᵃ15
ὑψηλότερος 5ᵃ12

φανερός 4ᵇ22, 5ᵃ21, 8ᵇ10
φάρυγξ 11ᵃ10
φθαρτά, τὰ 4ᵃ16
φθείρειν 6ᵃ8, 14
φθορά 10ᵇ3
φορά 5ᵃ16, 9ᵇ25, 10ᵃ18
φρονεῖν 6ᵃ19, 9ᵇ5
φύειν 9ᵇ24
φυσικός 10ᵃ8   φυσικὴν ὄρεξιν 5ᵃ24
φύσις 4ᵃ17, 7ᵃ5, 8ᵃ22, 9ᵃ13, ᵇ20,
10ᵃ2, ᵇ22, 11ᵇ26   ἡ ... τῆς φύσεως (sc. θεωρία) 4ᵃ3   κοινωνία
πρὸς ἄλληλα τοῖς τε νοητοῖς καὶ τοῖς
τῆς φύσεως 4ᵃ11   οὐδεμίαν ἔχειν
φύσιν 4ᵇ2   συνάπτειν τοῖς τῆς
φύσεως 4ᵇ3   ἀρχῆς φύσιν ἐχούσας
4ᵇ9   ἡ δὲ φ. ἐν κινήσει 4ᵇ20
τοῖς τῆς φύσεως αἰτία 4ᵇ23   ἡ τοῦ
ὀρεκτοῦ φ. 5ᵃ2   ὡρισμέναι ...
ἑκάστων αἱ φύσεις 7ᵃ18   τὴν τοῦ
παντὸς φύσιν 8ᵇ8   τοῖς πρώτοις
... τῆς φύσεως 10ᵃ6   τὸ ...
κινεῖσθαι ... τῆς φύσεως οἰκεῖον
10ᵃ10   παρὰ φύσιν 10ᵇ15   τὴν
φύσιν (εἰκὸς) ἐν ἅπασιν ὀρέγεσθαι
τοῦ ἀρίστου 11ᵃ5   τὰ τῆς φύσεως
11ᵃ21   τὴν τοῦ ὅλου φύσιν 11ᵇ6
φυτά 7ᵃ22, 8ᵇ27, 9ᵃ14, 10ᵃ5, 13,
ᵇ21   φυτῶν ... γενέσεις 7ᵇ4
φῶς 8ᵇ15 (bis)
φωτεινότατα, τὰ 9ᵇ13

χαλεπός 4ᵇ17, 7ᵃ19, 9ᵇ16   χαλεπώ-
τερος 9ᵃ26
χάριν adv. οὗ χ. 5ᵃ17   τούτων
χ. 10ᵇ20   κόσμου χ. 11ᵃ13   τὸ
τινὸς χ. 11ᵇ15
χεῖν 7ᵃ14
χεῖρον, τό. εἰς τὸ χ. ἡ μετάβασις 7ᵇ8
σχεδὸν ἰσομοιρεῖ τὸ χ. τῷ βελτίονι
8ᵃ24
χρῆσθαι 8ᵇ6
χρόνος 6ᵇ3
χώρα 5ᵇ22   τὴν τοῦ μέσου χώραν
11ᵃ24
χωρίζειν 4ᵃ12, 10ᵃ15
χωρίς 8ᵃ27

ψῆφος 6ᵃ20
ψυχή 6ᵃ2   ἡ ἔφεσις ... μετὰ ψυχῆς
5ᵇ1   ψυχῇ ... ἅμα δοκεῖ καὶ κίνησις ὑπάρχειν 5ᵇ3   αἱ αἰσθήσεις ...
ἐν ψυχῇ γίνονται 5ᵇ7   κρεῖττον
... ἡ τῆς ψυχῆς (sc. κίνησις) 5ᵇ9

ὥρα. τὰς ὥρας τὰς ἐτησίους 7ᵇ3
ὡς εἰπεῖν 7ᵃ16, 18, 11ᵇ4   ὡς ἁπλῶς
εἰ. 4ᵇ20
ὥσπερ explicative 4ᵃ11, 5ᵇ18, 6ᵃ14,
10ᵇ7
ὥσπερ ἂν εἰ 4ᵇ15
ὥστε in apodosi 5ᵃ20
ὠφελεῖσθαι (10ᵇ12)

INDEX TO THE INTRODUCTION AND COMMENTARY[1]

Alcmaeon 5ᵃ4
Anacoluthon 7ᵇ15
Analysis xi–xviii (see also 41)
Anaxagoras 11ᵃ22
Andronicus ix–x
Ardea cinerea 10ᵇ15
Aristotle:
  Hesychius' and Diogenes' lists of works of ix
  Περὶ ἀρχῆς ascribed to by Hermippus x
  reminiscences of in T. 4ᵃ4, 13–16, 5ᵃ2, 27, 6ᵃ1, 19–22, ᵇ3–4, 5, 6–9, 13, 21, 9ᵃ18, ᵇ6, 8, 10, 11–13, 15, 21, 10ᵃ8, 13, ᵇ9, 10, 12, 15, 11ᵃ9–11, 11–12, 19–21, 22, ᵇ9
  prime mover moves by being object of desire 5ᵃ2, 16, 25–8
  classification of movements 5ᵃ16, 23
  theory of prime mover xxv, 5ᵇ3, 12, 6ᵃ1, 7ᵇ15, 22–3, 23, 10ᵃ1, 6, 19–20
  approximations to a doctrine of divine providence 6ᵃ1
  work on the philosophy of Archytas 6ᵃ19–22
  view of the indefinite dyad 6ᵃ25
  interpretation of Platonic 'great and small' 6ᵃ25
  criticism of Speusippus for failure to give coherent account of genesis of material world 6ᵇ5
  his account of Xenocrates compared with those of T. and Sextus Empiricus 6ᵇ6–9
  interpretation of Parmenides' Way of Opinion 6ᵇ25
  recognized both formal and material principles 7ᵃ6–7
  belief in spontaneous generation 7ᵃ18
  belief in static and unchanging first principles 7ᵇ10
  opposition to Pythagorean doctrine of good and evil principles 8ᵃ22

Meteorol. 10ᵃ4
  distinction between method of metaphysics and that of natural philosophy 10ᵃ8
Arrangement xviii–xxiii
Atomists:
  κινήσεως ἀρχή is τὸ αὐτὸ κινοῦν 5ᵃ4
  doctrine of void 8ᵇ6–8
  indefinite variety of atoms 11ᵇ21–3
Authorship ix–x

Bessarion 1

Callimachus 7ᵃ14
Camotius xi
Cicero xxvi
Clement of Alexandria xxvi
Commentary by Camotius xi
Conflation, Usener's theory of xxiii–xxiv
Constructio ad sensum 4ᵇ9, 5ᵃ27, 6ᵇ3–4, 8ᵃ2

Dative:
  of reference 10ᵇ12, 25, 11ᵇ2–7
  of respect 7ᵃ12, 10ᵇ23
Diagonals 6ᵃ25
Diogenes Laertius ix–x, 6ᵇ5
Dislocation of text xix–xxiii

Earth:
  regarded as a first principle 6ᵇ25
  perhaps treated as the primary element by Xenophanes 6ᵇ25
Editions x–xi
Ellipse 5ᵃ27, ᵇ27, 6ᵇ16, 7ᵇ15, 8ᵃ12, 11ᵇ1, 2–7
Epicurus 10ᵃ8
Epinomis 6ᵃ25
Eurysus 6ᵃ19–22
Eurytus 6ᵃ19–22
Evil 11ᵃ19–21

Final cause 7ᵃ23
First principles 5ᵃ10–13, 7ᵃ15–19, 19–ᵇ5
  their validity to be verified by deducing from them actual contents of universe 6ᵃ14

---

[1] This index is simply supplementary to the *Index Verborum*.

INTRODUCTION AND COMMENTARY INDEX 85

in metaphysics opp. mathematical sciences 6^{b}19
in the arts 7^{a}5
static and unchanging 7^{b}10

Geometrical objects 5^{a}26

Haplography 5^{a}25, 11^{b}12
Heavens:
  perhaps coeval with soul according to Plato 6^{b}3-4
  generated simultaneously with time according to Plato 6^{b}3-4
  Xenocrates' notion of 6^{b}6-9
Heraclitus 6^{b}25
Hermippus ix-x
Hermodorus 6^{a}25
Hesiod 6^{b}25
Hesychius ix
Hiatus xxxii
Hippasus 6^{b}25

Ideas:
  existence of denied by Speusippus 4^{a}18
  Plato's theory of 4^{b}6, 6^{b}13
  mathematical numbers identified by Xenocrates with 6^{b}6-9
Identity 8^{b}25
Iliad 5^{b}17
Infinitive 9^{b}11-13
Ion of Chios 7^{a}14
Irrational roots 6^{a}25
Itacism 5^{b}6

Lacunae, Usener's theory of xix-xxiii

Magnitudes:
  Plato's classification of 6^{a}26
  generation of, according to Speusippus 6^{a}26
  classification and derivation of, according to Xenocrates 6^{a}26
Manuscripts:
  enumerated and described xxvi-xxvii
  errors of archetype xxvii-xxviii
  interrelations of xxviii-xxxii
  orthography xxxii

Neuter gender, T.'s reversion to in referring to anything inanimate 5^{a}25, 6^{b}16, 19
Nicolaus of Damascus ix
Numbers:
  generation of 6^{a}25, 28
  Plato's theory of, opp. spatial magnitudes 6^{a}28

Plato's derivation of soul from 6^{a}28
mathematical numbers identified by Xenocrates with Ideas 6^{b}6-9
in Plato's theory of Ideas 6^{b}13

Parmenides 6^{b}25
Philolaus 6^{a}19-22
Philoponus 11^{b}1
Planes 6^{a}26
Plato:
  reminiscences of in T. 4^{a}4, 5^{a}4, 6^{a}28, ^{b}3-4, 21
  Ideas prior to objects of mathematics 4^{b}6
  κινήσεως ἀρχή is τὸ αὐτὸ κινοῦν 5^{a}4
  probably familiar with method later used by Theo Smyrnaeus for approximating to $\sqrt{2}$ 6^{a}25
  classification of numbers in *Theaetetus* 6^{a}25
  'ideal magnitudes' opp. 'mathematical magnitudes' 6^{a}26
  doctrine of χώρα or τύπος 6^{a}28
  reference by Aristotle to ἄγραφα δόγματα of 6^{a}28
  identification of τὸ μεθεκτικόν with τὸ μέγα καὶ τὸ μικρόν 6^{a}28
  identification of τὰ ἄπειρα with τὸ μέγα καὶ τὸ μικρόν 6^{a}28
  numbers opp. spatial magnitudes 6^{a}28
  derivation of soul from numbers 6^{a}28
  perhaps made soul coeval with heavens 6^{b}3-4
  generated time and heavens simultaneously 6^{b}3-4
  theory of Ideas 6^{b}13, 11^{b}19
  belief in static and unchanging first principles 7^{b}10
  criticized by T. 9^{b}21
Plato and the Platonists 7^{a}6-7
  impossibility of exact study of nature 4^{a}4
  derivation of sensible world from the One or from numbers 5^{a}25-8
  this derivation incompatible with doctrine that sensible things are in movement 5^{a}25
  generation of numbers 6^{a}25
  generation of planes and solids 6^{a}26
Pliny the Elder 10^{b}15
Pre-Socratics 7^{a}6-7
Proclus 6^{a}25

Pythagoreans 7ᵃ6-7
   κινήσεως ἀρχή is τὸ αὐτὸ κινοῦν 5ᵃ4
   Alcmaeon's agreement with 5ᵃ4
   derivation of sensible world from the One or from numbers 5ᵃ25-8
   representation of numbers by geometrical forms 6ᵃ19-22
   cosmology 6ᵇ25
   doctrine of good and evil principles 8ᵃ22
   doctrine of central fire 11ᵃ23-5
   Speusippus' agreement with 11ᵃ23-5

Rational fractions 6ᵃ25
Rhinthon 7ᵃ14

Sextus Empiricus 6ᵇ6-9
Simplicius 6ᵃ25
Solids 6ᵃ26
Sophron 7ᵃ14
Soul:
   a φύσις αὐτοκίνητος according to Alcmaeon 5ᵃ4
   derived by Plato from numbers 6ᵃ28
   perhaps coeval with heavens in *Timaeus* 6ᵇ3-4
Speusippus:
   mathematical objects the primary realities 4ᵃ18
   generation of magnitudes 6ᵃ26
   criticized by Aristotle for failure to give coherent account of genesis of material world 6ᵇ5
   doctrine that good is not a primary principle 11ᵃ23-5

Spontaneous generation 7ᵃ18
Substances 6ᵇ6-9

Theo Smyrnaeus 6ᵃ25
Theophrastus:
   Hermippus', Diogenes', and Andronicus' lists of works of ix-x
   Περὶ τῶν ἁπλῶν διαπορημάτων x
   probably never wrote substantive work on metaphysics xxiv
   competence in metaphysics xxiv-xxv
   positive suggestions made by xxv-xxvi
   confusion of natural science with its subject-matter 4ᵃ5-6
   his account of Xenocrates compared with those of Aristotle and Sextus Empiricus 6ᵇ6-9
   references to *Physicae Opiniones* 6ᵇ25, 8ᵇ6-8, 9ᵇ21
Time 6ᵇ3-4
Title ix-x
Tyrannio xxiv

Void 8ᵇ6-8

Xenocrates:
   Ideas identical with mathematical objects 4ᵃ18, 6ᵇ6-9
   probably derived geometrical objects from numbers 5ᵃ26
   perhaps originated phrase ἀόριστος δυάς 6ᵃ24
   classification and derivation of magnitudes 6ᵃ26
   his hierarchy of substances 6ᵇ6-9
   notion of the heavens 6ᵇ6-9
Xenophanes 6ᵇ25

ἀκαριαῖος 11ᵃ18
ἅμα opp. ἄμα xxxii, 5ᵃ12
ἄμετρα 6ᵃ25
ἄν iterative 8ᵇ23
ἀντιμεταλλακτέον 7ᵇ13
ἀξιόχρεως with genitive 4ᵃ20
ἀόριστος δυάς. origin and meaning of phrase 6ᵃ24, 25   Plato's doctrine of 6ᵃ28
ἅπαυτος 5ᵃ3
ἄπειρα, τὰ 6ᵃ28
ἀριθμοί, διαμετρικοί 6ᵃ25   ἑτερομήκεις 6ᵃ25   ἰσόπλευροι 6ᵃ25   πλευρικοί 6ᵃ25   προμήκεις 6ᵃ25   τετράγωνοι 6ᵃ25
ἄρρητα 6ᵃ25

βάθος 6ᵃ25

γε corrupted to τε 11ᵇ18
γίνομαι opp. γίγνομαι xxxii
γραμμαί 6ᵃ25

δυνάμεις 6ᵃ25

εἶ abbreviation for εἶναι 11ᵃ20
ἐμφαίνει transitive 11ᵃ14
ἐν 'contained in', 'depending on' 8ᵃ23
ἐπί with κατ' ἀναλογίαν 8ᵃ19
ἐπιμιμεῖσθαι 11ᵇ1
ἕτερα 8ᵇ17 f.
ἐτήσιοι opp. ἐτησίαι 7ᵇ3

AND COMMENTARY 87

in sense of πλήν 5ᵃ4
ᾗ καί 9ᵇ1

λογῶδες 7ᵇ18

μέγα (τὸ) καὶ τὸ μικρόν 6ᵃ28
μεθεκτικόν, τὸ 6ᵃ28
μὲν οὖν corrective 11ᵃ25
μῆκη 6ᵃ25

ν paragogicum xxxii

ὁμοίως, Theophrastean construction of 5ᵃ25
οὐθείς opp. οὐδείς xxxii

πέλλος 10ᵇ15
περιτιθέναι 6ᵇ7
πλάτος 6ᵃ25
πλέον opp. πλεῖον xxxii

στράγξ 7ᵃ14

τὰ μὲν . . . τὰ δέ adverbial 9ᵃ8-9
τε by corruption from γε 11ᵇ18
τόπος 6ᵃ28

χώρα 6ᵃ28

ὥστε doubled 4ᵇ2   *in apodosi* 5ᵃ20

NOTES

NOTES

NOTES

NOTES

Some Books of similar interest...

ANCIENT AUTHORS, COMMENTARIES
AND HISTORIOGRAPHY

Aelian, *Varia Historia*
Arrian, *Taktika/Expedition Against the Alans*
Festus Rufus Avienus, *Ora Maritima*
G. L. Barber, The Historian Ephorus
T. S. Brown, Onesicritus
G. Coedes, Textes d'Auteurs Grecs et Latines Relatifs a l'Extreme Orient
A. Couat, Alexandrian Poetry under the First Three Ptolemies, 324-222 BC
R. M. Dawkins, Nature of the Cypriot Chronicle of Leontios Makharias
Hanno the Carthaginian, *Periplus* (of Africa) 3rd ed.
G. Hyde, De Olympionicarum Statuis a Pausania Commemoratis
Isidore of Charax, Parthian Stations
Justin, History of Macedonia under Philip II
    and Alexander the Great (Books VII to XII)
H. S. Jones, Ancient Writers on Greek Sculpture
Marinos of Neapolis, Life of Proclus
    and Commentary on the *Dedomena* of Euclid
K. Mueller, Fragments of the Lost Historians of Alexander the Great
A. D. Nock, Sallustius: *Concerning the Gods and The Universe*
C. Odahl, Early Christian Latin Literature
Philon & Heron, Artillery & Siegecraft in Antiquity
Polybius and Ps.-Hyginus, The Fortification of the Roman Camp
Polyaenus, Strategems of War, 2 vols, edd. P. Krentz and E. Wheeler
J. U. Powell, *Collectanea Alexandrina*
C H. Roseman, Pytheas of Massilia, *On the Ocean*
C. A. Robinson, Alexander the Great
    & The *Ephemerides* of Alexander's Expedition
Stephanos Byzantinos, *Ethnikon*
E. H. Sturtevant, The Pronunciation of Greek and Latin
E. A. Thompson, A Roman Reformer and Inventor
E. M. Thompson, A Handbook of Greek and Latin Paleography
T. G. Tucker, Etymological Dictionary of Latin
C. B. Welles, Royal Correspondence in the Hellenistic Period
E. R. Wharton, Etymological Lexicon of Classical Greek
U. Wilamowitz-Moellendorf, Greek Historical Writing and Apollo
E. G. Wilkins, *Know Thyself* in Greek and Latin Literature

ANCIENT WARFARE

J. G. DeVoto, Arrian, *Taktika:* A Manual for Ancient Warfare
G. H. Chase, Shield Devices of the Ancient Greeks
G. L. Cheesman, The Auxilia of the Roman Imperial Army
G. T. Griffith, The Mercenaries of the Hellenistic World
H. P. Judson, Caesar's Army, 2nd ed. with a New Bibliography
F. A. Lepper, Trajan's Parthian War (with the fragments of Arrian's *Parthica*)
H. W. Parke, Greek Mercenary Soldiers
H. M. D. Parker, The Roman Legions
Philon & Heron, Artillery and Siegecraft in Antiquity
Polyaenus, Strategems of War, 2 vols, edd. P. Krentz and E. Wheeler
Polybius and Ps.-Hyginus, The Fortifications of the Roman Camp,
        edd. M. C. J. Miller and James G. DeVoto
T. C. Sarikakis, The Hoplite General in Athens
C. G. Starr, The Roman Imperial Navy 31 B. C.-A. D. 324 (3rd ed.)
W. W. Tarn, Hellenistic Military & Naval Developments

ROMAN HISTORY

W. T. Arnold, Roman Provincial Administration
L. Bolchazy, Hospitality in Antiquity (formerly Hospitality in Early Rome)
J. B. Bury & C. Cobham, Supplement to the History of the Later Roman Empire
        (976-1057 AD) and bound with Patriarchs of Constantinople
M. P. Charlesworth, Trade Routes and Commerce of the Roman Empire
G. F. Hill, Historical Roman Coins
F. Hirth, China and the Roman Orient
J. G. Milne, A History of Egypt under Roman Rule
J. G. Milne, Surgical Instruments in Greek and Roman Times
Th. Mommsen, The Provinces of the Roman Empire, 2 vols
M. P. Nilsson, Imperial Rome
L. R. Taylor, The Cults of Ostia
E. J. Urch, Evolution of the Inquisitorial Procedure in Roman Law

ATHLETICS

E. N. Gardiner, Athletics of the Ancient World
G. Hyde, De Olympicarum Statuis a Pausania Commemoratis
T. Klee, Zur Geschichte der Gymnischen Agone an Griechischen Festen
R. Knab, Die Periodoniken
S. Miller, Arete
R. Robinson, Sources for the History of Greek Athletics
I. Rutgers, List of Olympian Victors
T. F. Scanlon, Greek and Roman Athletics: A Bibliography
D. C. Young, The Olympic Myth of Greek Amateur Athletics

Books of related interest....

H. I. Bell
Cults and Creeds in Graeco-Roman Egypt
E. R. Bevan
Stoics and Sceptics
C. Bryan
Ancient Egyptian Medicine: The Papyrus Ebers
E. A. W. Budge
Herb Doctors in the Ancient World. The Divine Origin of the Herbalist
F. H. Cramer
Astrology in Roman Law and Politics
E. R. Dodds
Select Passages Illustrating Neoplatonism
D. R. Dudley
History of Cynicism
L. Edelstein
The Hippocratic Oath
L. R. Farnell
Greek Hero Cults
J. B. Hurry
Imhotep: The Egyptian God of Medicine
W. H. S. Jones
Philosophy and Medicine in Ancient Greece
C. D. Leake
The Old Egyptian Medical Papyrus: Papyrus Hearst
Marinos of Neapolis
Life of Proclus and Commentary on the *Dedomena* of Euclid
J. G. Milne
Surgical Instruments in Greek and Roman Times
A. D. Nock
Sallustius: *Concerning the Gods and the Universe*
D. L. O'Leary
How Greek Science Passed to the Arabs
J. E. Raven
Pythagoreans and Eleatics
W. D. Ross & F. H. Fobes
Theophrastus *Metaphysics:* Translation, Commentary and Introduction
L. R. Taylor
The Cults of Ostia
T. Taylor
Proclus the Neoplatonic Philosopher: Two Treatises
A. Walton
Asklepios: The Cult of the Greek God of Medicine
E. G. Wilkins
Know Thyself in Greek and Latin Literature

Ancient Athens and Greece

W. S. Ferguson
Hellenistic Athens
J. E. Harrison
Primitive Athens as Described by Thucydides
B. V. Head & W. R. Roberts
Ancient Boeotians and the Coinage of Ancient Boeotia
G. F. Hill
Historical Greek Coins
O. Jahn & A. Michaelis
Acropolis of Athens as Described by Pausanias (and other writers)
J. Kirchner
Prosopographia Attica, 2 vols
J. O. Lofberg
Sycophancy in Athens
A. Milchhoefer
Ancient Athens, Piraeus and Phaleron: Literary and Epigraphical Testimonia
A. Mommsen
Athenae Christianae
D. L. O'Leary
How Greek Science Passed to the Arabs
H. Pope
Foreigners in Attic Inscriptions and Non-Athenians in Attic Inscriptions
P. Poralla
Prosopographia Lacaedaemoniorum
B. Powell
Athenian Mythology: Erechthonius and the Three Daughters of Cecrops
Wm. Ramsay
Asianic Elements in Greek Civilization
L. C. Reilly
Slaves in Ancient Greece
T. C. Sarikakis, The Hoplite General in Athens
C. J. Schwenk
Athens in the Age of Alexander
Ch. Seltman
Athens: Its History and Coinage Before the Persian Invasion
J. Svoronos
Corpus of the Ancient Coins of Athens
M. N. Tod
Sidelights on Greek History
K. F. Vickery
Food in Early Greece
Th. Zielinski
The Religion of Greece

Printed in the United States
83876LV00009B/113/A